Financial Resilience and the Sustainable Development Goals

Financial resilience is a concept that is gaining importance in the context of Environmental, Social and Governance (ESG) risk and can be considered from the perspective of any entity operating in the market economy, from households to local government units. This book presents the concept of financial resilience from a global and an international perspective, and through the prism of the Sustainable Development Goals (SDGs).

It covers a broad spectrum, from the theoretical framework and the assessment of the current state of knowledge and research to the practical approach used in financial institutions. The book's key contribution is that it examines the link between the SDGs and financial resilience, which is an interesting and under-researched observation. Its original and innovative approach to financial resilience fills this research gap and also includes a discussion of artificial intelligence (AI) and digitalisation.

The book provides empirical analyses, case studies and a framework, strategies and recommendations for building financial resilience. As such, it will be a valuable source of knowledge for students, academics, researchers and policymakers in the field of finance, and particularly green and sustainable finance.

Magdalena Zioło is a full professor of Finance at the University of Szczecin, Poland. Her research and teaching focus on finance, banking and sustainability. She is the author and editor of numerous books, mostly about financing sustainable development.

Bruno S. Sergi is a professor of Political Economy at the University of Messina in Italy and concurrently serves as an instructor at Harvard University in the United States.

Routledge Focus on Economics and Finance

The fields of economics are constantly expanding and evolving. This growth presents challenges for readers trying to keep up with the latest important insights. Routledge Focus on Economics and Finance presents short books on the latest big topics, linking in with the most cutting-edge economics research.

Individually, each title in the series provides coverage of a key academic topic, whilst collectively the series forms a comprehensive collection across the whole spectrum of economics.

International Trade, Regulation and the Global Economy
The Impact of Anti-Competitive Market Distortions
Shanker A. Singham

The Digital Transformation of Banking
Bilal Sucubaşı, Andrijana Bojadzievska Danevska, Savica Dimitrieska and Elena Parnardzieva Stanoevska

The Circular Economy and SMEs
Edited by Fahimeh Khatami

Financial Security and Household Life Insurance
Bridging the Gap
Joanna Dębicka and Anna Jędrzychowska

Corporate Short-Term Financing in Europe
The Role of Trade Credit and Bank Loans in Liquidity Management
Julia Koralun-Bereźnicka

Financial Resilience and the Sustainable Development Goals
Edited by Magdalena Zioło and Bruno S. Sergi

For more information about this series, please visit: www.routledge.com/Routledge-Focus-on-Economics-and-Finance/book-series/RFEF

Financial Resilience and the Sustainable Development Goals

Edited by Magdalena Zioło
and Bruno S. Sergi

Routledge
Taylor & Francis Group
LONDON AND NEW YORK

First published 2026
by Routledge
4 Park Square, Milton Park, Abingdon, Oxon OX14 4RN

and by Routledge
605 Third Avenue, New York, NY 10158

Routledge is an imprint of the Taylor & Francis Group, an informa business

British Library Cataloguing-in-Publication Data
A catalogue record for this book is available from the British Library

ISBN: 978-1-041-09182-0 (hbk)
ISBN: 978-1-041-09185-1 (pbk)
ISBN: 978-1-003-64884-0 (ebk)

DOI: 10.4324/9781003648840

Typeset in Times New Roman
by SPi Technologies India Pvt Ltd (Straive)

Contents

List of figures *vii*
List of tables *viii*
List of contributors *ix*
Acknowledgement *xiii*

1 **Introduction** 1
MAGDALENA ZIOŁO AND BRUNO S. SERGI

2 **Concept and measurement of financial resilience** 6
KRZYSZTOF KLUZA

3 **Financial resilience of financial institutions** 26
EWA KULINSKA-SADŁOCHA

4 **Sustainable Development Goals (SDGs) and financial resilience in the EU-27: Romania's regions of development – A case study and policy insights** 45
DIANA-MIHAELA ȚÎRCĂ, ISABEL NOVO-CORTI, CORNELIA DUMITRU, AND XOSE PICATOSTE

5 **ESG and financial resilience** 70
FILIPPO GRASSO AND DANIELE SCHILIRÒ

6 **Building financial resilience** 86
MARTA POSTUŁA AND WOJCIECH CHMIELEWSKI

7 Conclusion 112
BRUNO S. SERGI

Index *113*

Figures

2.1 Financial resilience framework – process flowchart 13
3.1 Elements of resilience of financial institutions 28
3.2 A holistic approach to financial resilience regulation 33
4.1 SDG financing and the financial resilience of financial institutions 50
4.2 Geopolitical threats and geopolitical acts over the period 2010–2025 51
4.3 Cyberattacks by threat actor type 52
4.4 Decent work and economic growth according to national circumstances 55
4.5 SDG index score 56
4.6 Leave no one behind index score 57
4.7 Evolution of key indicators for the Romanian regions of development over the period 2021–2023 59
4.8 k-means clustering of regions with estimate of the financial resilience and sustainability by Fintech proxy 64
6.1 Evolution of financial regulations: Key milestones 2008–2025 90
6.2 Fintech investments and cybersecurity incidents in financial services (2020–2024) 94
6.3 Conceptual framework of AI's influence on institutional financial resilience 95

Tables

2.1 Description of the most popular financial resilience indicators 15
2.2 Metrics and RAG thresholds for the most popular financial resilience indicators 17
3.1 Determinants of financial institutions' resilience (synthetic view) 29
3.2 Examples of initiatives and regulations strengthening the resilience of financial institutions (global–regional–national–institutional levels) 34
3.3 Instruments and tools supporting financial resilience (synthetic view) 38
4.1 TFEU, SDGs, and key systemic areas 53
4.2 Analysis of intervention needs and SDGs on regions of development 60
4.3 Descriptive statistics 61
4.4 Principal component analysis 62
6.1 Risk Alignment Matrix and Strategies for Financial Resilience 89
6.2 Digital and Quantum Technologies and Financial Resilience: Comparative Overview 100
6.3 Comparative Analysis of Regulatory Approaches to Financial Resilience: USA, EU, and China 102

Contributors

Wojciech Chmielewski, PhD, is a research fellow at the Faculty of Management, University of Warsaw, specialising in corporate finance, R&D efficiency and the economic implications of innovation. His scientific work focuses on the relationship between R&D expenditure, labour market performance and macroeconomic outcomes in the European Union, with particular emphasis on the Information and Communication Technology (ICT) sector. He is the author and co-author of several peer-reviewed research articles published in international academic outlets. Alongside his academic activity, he serves as a Director at Bank Gospodarstwa Krajowego, where he is responsible for international cooperation with global financial institutions, including international development banks.

Cornelia Dumitru is a PhD scientific researcher at the Institute of National Economy and the Research Institute for Quality of Life of the Romanian Academy. She has been involved in several projects regarding the structural reform of the Romanian economy over the first years of transition, financed by the Dutch Matra programmes, and continued to work with partners from the Netherlands, the United Kingdom, France and Ireland over the years. Her main interests are in institutional economics, with an emphasis on the economic institutions of the labour market, and labour market dynamics and policies, and in the New Institutional Sociology and socio-economics, with a particular interest in how the digital economy impacts the social contract. Other interests cover sustainable development, the Green Deal and developments in the sphere of Corporate Social Responsibility (CSR) and ESG.

Filippo Grasso is a professor of Market Analysis at the University of Messina. He specialises in issues related to the governance of tourism policies and is the delegate of the Rector of the University of Messina for "scientific initiatives in the tourism sector".

Krzysztof Kluza (dr hab.) works at the Department of Quantitative Economics, Warsaw School of Economics (SGH), Poland. He does research in risk, strategy and change management, regional development, public finance, ESG and sustainable finance. He has over 25 years of professional experience in the manufacturing and financial sectors in various expert and managerial positions, including in the roles of CFO, CEO and General Manager in large corporations. He holds a CIMA professional qualification.

Ewa Kulińska-Sadłocha holds a PhD in economics and finance. She is a lecturer and an author and co-author of many publications, with a focus on finance, controlling, cost accounting and sustainability. She has more than 20 years of experience in teaching and conducting business trainings, as well as extensive experience in business practice: banking, accounting and controlling, including being an advisor on the implementation of sustainable practices for business. She is a member of the Editorial Committee of the journal *Safe Bank*, Scientific Council of the Polish Economic Society and Committee for the Partnership Agreement on EU funds 2021–2027 with Poland.

Isabel Novo-Corti is a full professor of Economic Analysis at Universidade da Coruña (UDC-Spain) and has a PhD in economics. She is the coordinator of the EDaSS research group on Economic Development and Social Sustainability, director of the University Institute of Maritime Studies and was the head of the department of Economic Analysis and Business Administration at the UDC. She is the director of the *Atlantic Review of Economics*. Her research focuses on public policies and sustainability in the framework of Knowledge Society and Labour Market. She has published in prestigious academic journals such as the *Journal of Cleaner Production*, *Ocean & Coastal Management*, *Marine Pollution Bulletin* and *Computers in Human Behavior*. She has been a visiting scholar at Washington University (Missouri, USA), Reading (United Kingdom) and Harvard University (Massachusetts, USA). She has been honoured with international awards such as the best work on ethical economy at the International Conference XXII Hispanic-Portuguese Scientific Management Conference in Vila Real (Portugal, 2012), and the award for best research paper of 2015 published in the journal *Management of Environmental Quality*. She has been invited as a keynote speaker at several international conferences and participated in numerous research projects, at both national and international levels.

Xose Picatoste is an assistant professor of Economics at the University of A Coruña (UDC), Spain. He is a member of the inter-university research group ECOBAS and also the research group on Economic

Development and Social Sustainability (EDaSS); he collaborates as a member of the SET-LASE research group on the socio-economics of labour at the Autonomous University of Madrid (UAM). He was a recognised student at Oxford University, and nowadays he is a member of the Oxford Alumni. He got his PhD at the Universidad Autónoma de Madrid. His research is framed in socio-economics and sustainability, in particular, the labour market, poverty, social exclusion and ICT. Picatoste has published widely in prestigious journals, received awards for his research and presented at numerous international conferences, while also serving as a guest editor for academic journals.

Marta Postuła is the head of the Finance and Accounting department at the Faculty of Management, University of Warsaw, Warsaw, Poland.

Daniele Schilirò is associate professor of Economics, Department of Economics, University of Messina. He did his B.A. (Laurea) in Economics, Catholic University of Milan, 1979, and M.Phil programme in Political Economy at the University of Cambridge (UK), 1979/1980. He was a special graduate student at the University of Yale (USA), 1980. Schilirò is the winner of the Scholarship "Bonaldo Stringher", Bank of Italy, Rome, 1980. He is a researcher and member of the Scientific Committee of the Centre of Research in Economic Analysis (CRANEC), Catholic University of Milan. He was also a research scholar in macroeconomics, economics of structural change and history of economic analysis at the Universities of Cambridge (Selwyn College, 1985) and (Sidney Sussex College, 2002) and University of Oxford (Brasenose College, 1986) (U.K.), University of Twente (NL), 2006. Schilirò was a visiting professor at the University of Dubai (UAE), 2014, and University of Valencia (ES), 2016 and 2017. He is also a conference speaker and panellist at several International Forums and Meetings and a member of the editorial board of *Frontiers in Management Research* (Isaac Scientific Publishing) and *Economics* (Science Publishing Group) and *Journal of Mathematical Economics and Finance* (Asers Publishing). His current research interests include growth, innovation, SMEs, green economy, EMU governance, Gulf economies and behavioural economics.

Bruno S. Sergi is a professor of Political Economy at the University of Messina in Italy and concurrently serves as an instructor at Harvard University in the United States.

Diana-Mihaela Țîrcă, PhD, is a professor at the University of Bucharest, Faculty of Administration and Business, Department of Business Administration. Her research area is economic, social and environmental sustainability, green economy, labour market dynamics and migration. She has participated as a visiting professor at the University of Szczecin, Poland, and in research internships at the University of A Coruna, Spain, and the University of Salerno, Italy. She is a guest editor of the special issue on Sustainability Energy Use and Management (*Progress in Industrial Ecology, An International Journal*, 2015), special issue – Innovation for Sustainable Development (*Journal for Cleaner Production*, 2018), special issue – Information Society and Sustainable Development – Selected Papers from the 5th International Conference ISSD 2018 (*Sustainability*, 2019), Economic Inequality, Regional Disparities and Sustainable Development (*Sustainability*, 2021), Impact of Sustainable Financial and Economic Development on Greenhouse Gas Emission (*Energies*, 2022) and Breakthroughs in Sustainable Energy and Economic Development (*Energies*, 2023).

Magdalena Zioło is a full professor of Finance at the University of Szczecin, Poland. Her research and teaching focus on finance, banking and sustainability. She is the author and editor of numerous books, mostly about financing sustainable development.

Acknowledgement

I would like to thank the reviewer, dr hab. Zbysław Dobrowolski, prof University of Zielona Góra, for valuable and constructive comments and suggestions.

1 Introduction

Magdalena Ziolo and Bruno S. Sergi

Financial resilience is a concept that is gaining importance in the context of Environmental, Social, and Governance (ESG) risk. Financial resilience can be considered from the perspective of any entity operating in the market economy, from households to local government units. Financial resilience is an essential issue because it informs about a given entity's resilience to shocks, particularly the ability to absorb shocks and rebuild financial stability. Financial resilience is understood as

> The ability of a financial market or financial system to effectively withstand and quickly recover from external shocks (Vegt et al., 2015). Therefore, financial resilience characteristics should include the following two primary aspects: the ability to absorb shocks and the ability to recover from shocks (Broto & Lamas, 2020). Furthermore, the above definitions and explorations regarding resilience all involve external shocks. Indeed, some scholars have started to empirically study resilience from the perspective of shocks (Fingleton et al., 2012; Lucas et al., 2018), but there is still a lack of systematic resilience measurement framework.

Most of the works published in the field of financial resilience focus on the problem of its measurement (Chen & Sun, 2024), the determinants of this phenomenon, and ways to counteract it, among others, through financial literacy and regulations (Andreou, Anyfantaki & Atkinson, 2023). Much attention is paid to financial resilience from the perspective of central banking (CEP Policy, 2024) and households (McKnight, Abigail, & Marc Rucci, 2020). Financial institutions are particularly important in terms of financial resilience because, on the one hand, they affect the financial resilience of other entities due to their mission and the role they play in the economy in terms of ensuring security, stability, and trust, and on the other hand, they are themselves subject to the impact of risks and factors that affect their financial resilience. Therefore, the question arises as to how the financial resilience of financial institutions can be

DOI: 10.4324/9781003648840-1

built and strengthened; on the one hand, these are actions directly related to these institutions, for example, regulations, and on the other hand, actions related to building financial resilience on the part of clients of the financial sector. Therefore, the proposal aims to present the problem of financial resilience from the global and international perspective of financial institutions and their environment—in particular, to assess how financial institutions acquire financial resilience and to which factors this resilience is the weakest.

The monograph aims to present the phenomenon of financial resilience from a global and international perspective. In particular, it is assumed that the evolving role of the phenomenon and the need for a new perspective on it in the context of growing ESG risk and implemented policies in the field of sustainability should be shown through the prism of Sustainable Development Goals (SDGs). The scope of the monograph covers a broad spectrum, from the theoretical framework for the problem and showing the state of knowledge and research to presenting the practical approach used in financial institutions and from the side of their clients. The original context is to show the problem of financial resilience through the connections created at the interface of financial and non-financial institutions and the penetration of the resilience of institutions from both these sectors. An interesting and little-researched phenomenon is the connection between SDGs and financial resilience. SDGs are designed to support the achievement of sustainable development goals and reduce ESG risk, so it is worth diagnosing the connections between SDGs and the financial resilience of financial institutions. It is a research gap and the purpose of the book proposal. The book presents the state of knowledge on financial resilience, with a particular focus on financial institutions. The chapters present an original and innovative approach to financial resilience, analyzing this phenomenon regarding the impact of ESG and SDGs on them.

The monograph consists of seven chapters, including an introduction and conclusion, which contain valuable recommendations and tips for decision-makers involved in building the financial resilience of financial institutions. This chapter is the introduction and presents the justification for taking up the problem of financial resilience, justifies the research gap, and explains the original and innovative approach to presenting the problem of financial resilience from the perspective of financial institutions. This chapter will also present the purpose of the monograph, the content of its chapters, and the main conclusions from the considerations. Chapter 2 shows how financial resilience begins at the household level and scales to entire systems. For families, it means savings cushions, insurance coverages, clear financial literacy, and social networks that lend support when incomes falter. It hinges on capital buffers, liquidity reserves, and macroprudential tools for institutions. The concept draws on the life-cycle hypothesis and precautionary-saving theory, then borrows "resilience" from ecology's focus on adaptation within dynamic disturbances. Measurement has matured from a binary "Can you raise $2,000 in 30 days?" to multidimensional frameworks. Salignac et al. identify four pillars—economic resources, access, knowledge, and social capital—while the OECD defines five dimensions: control over money, expense management, financial buffers, stress-coping, and purposeful planning. Recent research on climate-related risks—disparate bank exposures, dynamic stress-testing, and the Climate Risk (CRISK) index—highlights artificial intelligence's (AI)'s ability to detect threats and speed up crisis responses. Future frontiers include digital currencies, embedded finance, and subscription-banking models, each demanding cross-disciplinary insights from economics, behavioral science, climate science, and computer science. Chapter 3 examines how banks, insurers, and markets must survive downturns and sustain lending, payment flows, insurance payouts, and capital-market intermediation. Internally, this requires substantial capital and liquidity ratios, diversified portfolios, stable income streams, sound governance, robust risk cultures, operational continuity plans, and ESG integration. Externally, institutions face macroeconomic swings, geopolitical tensions, sectoral linkages, demographic shifts, and climate hazards. Regulators, as the overseers of the financial system, have woven micro- and macroprudential strands—from Basel III/IV and Financial Stability Board (FSB) standards to EU rules (CRR/CRD, BRRD, Solvency II, EMIR, DORA)—with national regimes to reinforce buffers, resolution frameworks, and supervisory cooperation. They ensure institutions adhere to these standards and are prepared for potential shocks. Meanwhile, RegTech and SupTech tools powered by predictive analytics shift oversight from annual filings to near-continuous monitoring, curbing regulatory arbitrage. Lasting resilience demands parallel development of institutions and markets, high-quality disclosures, cross-border data sharing, policy alignment with the European Green Deal, and sustainable-transition strategies. Chapter 4 discusses embedding the UN's 17 Sustainable Development Goals into financial strategies, advancing global targets, and deepening institutional resilience. Across the EU-27, banks and funds must channel savings into renewable energy, infrastructures of inclusion, and tech-driven education, all while maintaining balance-sheet strength. Romania's eight development regions illustrate how local resilience relies on strong institutions, flexible public–private partnerships, and diversified portfolios. Two EU instruments stand out: the Savings and Investments Union, which empowers citizens to invest as little as €10 in long-term ventures via regulated providers, and the Digital Operational Resilience Act (DORA), which shores up Information and Communication Technology (ICT) defenses. This chapter proposes an integrated framework tailored to the digital economy, aligning economic, social, and environmental objectives. This chapter highlights the importance of building resilience and promoting societal goals through innovative institutional frameworks. By incorporating SDG and ESG principles at all levels of policy and operations, from the boardroom to local savings groups, we can foster significant and meaningful change. Chapter 5 describes how was once a values-oriented overlay has become a core strategic imperative. ESG criteria now drive capital allocation, risk management, and corporate reputation—key ingredients of resilience. Empirical studies link strong ESG performance, especially in banking, to higher efficiency, more stable cash flows, and enhanced brand premiums. ESG integration reduces environmental liabilities, fosters social trust, and reinforces governance transparency, all of which buffer firms against shocks. Yet realizing these benefits depends on standardized reporting frameworks—International Sustainability Standards Board (ISSB), Corporate Sustainability Reporting Directive (CSRD), Task Force on Climate-Related Financial Disclocures (TCFD)—and high-quality data. Fragmentation in methodologies and disparities in regulators' expectations impede comparability and hinder risk aggregation. Harmonizing metrics, bolstering corporate disclosure, and fostering collaboration among regulators, investors, and researchers are essential. When ESG is thoroughly woven into strategic planning and performance metrics, it ceases to be compliance overhead and becomes a competitive edge that cements long-term resilience. Chapter 6 delves into today's digital era, and resilience is inseparable from technology. Artificial intelligence and machine learning drive sophisticated early-warning systems that blend traditional financial ratios with alternative data—transaction flows, online sentiments, supply-chain signals—to spot vulnerabilities before they crystallize. Yet these innovations introduce new attack vectors: cyberthreats, data-privacy risks, third-party dependencies on cloud and fintech providers, and opacity in AI decision-making. Regulators have responded with tighter rules—Basel accords updated for operational tech risk, MiCA for crypto assets, and DORA for ICT disruptions—yet they must strike a delicate balance between oversight and innovation. Financial institutions must develop integrated resilience frameworks that unite capital management, operational risk, technology governance, and compliance into coherent strategic plans. Key pillars include initiative-taking scenario planning and AI-driven stress tests, rigorous third-party risk management, adaptive governance bodies with tech and ESG expertise, and innovation governance that fosters experimentation in sandboxes while maintaining strong controls. Only institutions that synchronize financial strength, digital capabilities, ESG integration, and dynamic governance will thrive amid uncertainty. Chapter 7 is the conclusion.

The monograph is addressed to practitioners and theoreticians dealing with finance, mainly green and sustainable finance. The monograph will be a valuable source of knowledge for students, teachers, lecturers, and PhD students.

On behalf of all the authors
Magdalena Ziolo, Bruno S. Sergi

References

Andreou, P. C., Anyfantaki, S., & Atkinson, A. (2023). Financial literacy for financial resilience: Evidence from Cyprus during the pandemic period. *Cyprus Economic Policy Review*, *17*(1), 27–54.

Brief, C. P. (2024). Financial resilience in an age of environmental change: Central banks and financial regulators feel the heat.

Broto, C., & Lamas, M. (2020). Is market liquidity less resilient after the financial crisis? Evidence for US Treasuries. *Economic Modelling*, *93*, 217–229.

Chen, Y., & Sun, C. (2024). A new method for measuring financial resilience. *Economics Letters*, 242, 111883.

Fingleton, B., Garretsen, H., & Martin, R. (2012). Recessionary shocks and regional employment: evidence on the resilience of UK regions. *Journal of Regional Science*, *52*(1), 109–133.

Lucas, I., Cotsaftis, M., & Bertelle, C. (2018). Self-organization, resilience and robustness of complex systems through an application to financial market from an agent-based approach. *International Journal of Bifurcation and Chaos*, *28*(03), 1850044.

McKnight, A., & Rucci, M. (2020). The financial resilience of households: 22 country study with new estimates, breakdowns by household characteristics and a review of policy options.

Van Der Vegt, G. S., Essens, P., Wahlström, M., & George, G. (2015). Managing risk and resilience. *Academy of Management Journal*, *58*(4), 971–980.

2 Concept and measurement of financial resilience

Krzysztof Kluza

2.1 Introduction and origin of the concept

Financial resilience describes the ability of individuals, households, organizations, or financial systems to absorb financial shocks, adapt to adverse changes, and return (or transition) to sustainable financial stability. At the household level, financial resilience means having savings, insurance, and access to appropriate financial products, as well as social support and financial literacy to manage debt, expenses, and risk. At the institutional and governmental levels, financial resilience means having adequate capital, liquidity, and macroprudential frameworks in place (IMF, 2023a; OECD, 2022; Salignac et al., 2019). The OECD/INFE and the World Bank generally measure financial resilience at the micro level (households) as the ability to cope with unexpected expenses (e.g., can you organize additional funds within 30 days, and where would you get them?). They treat it as a dimension of financial well-being. However, at the systemic level, resilience is the financial sector's ability to absorb losses and continue providing services during shocks, for example, through capital buffers or macroprudential tools. Since the 2008 financial crisis and the subsequent pandemic, the concept of financial resilience has gained particular importance (see ECB, 2023b; IMF, 2023b).

It should be noted from the beginning that the concept of financial resilience was originally associated with the behavior of individuals and households. This continues to be the dominant trend in research. In their analysis of research trends, Tahir and Richards (2025) indicate that studies are dominated by analyses based on the individual-related definition of financial resilience, which is defined as "Ability to raise funds in an emergency, access to financial resources (financial inclusion) and ability to bounce back at times of financial hardships" (Tahir and Richards, 2025, p. 10).

The theoretical foundations of the concept of financial resilience date back to the life-cycle hypothesis, whose theoretical foundations were proposed by Modigliani and Brumberg (1954). This theory posits that individuals plan their consumption and savings behavior throughout their life

DOI: 10.4324/9781003648840-2

cycle in order to maintain a stable standard of living. Modigliani and Brumberg argued that savings enable individuals to cope with crisis situations resulting from a temporary decline in income or an unexpected increase in expenses. Subsequently, in the 1960s and 1970s, the precautionary saving theory was developed, which became a key basis for the concept of financial resilience. Researchers such as Leland (1968) and Sandmo (1970) demonstrated that uncertainty about future income motivates individuals to reduce current consumption and increase savings as a safeguard against potential financial setbacks.

At the same time, the concept of financial resilience was enriched by the adoption of the term "resilience" from ecological sciences. In ecology, resilience has been shown to be not only about stability around equilibrium but also about the sustainability of relationships within a system despite disturbances (Holling, 1973). This approach then spread to the social sciences, crisis management, economics, and, after the 2008 financial crisis, finance.

The turn of the century brought a systematization of research on financial resilience. Carroll (1997) developed the theory of "buffer-stock" behavior, which shows that individuals with uncertain future incomes will maintain their consumption level within their current income, leading to a close link between consumption and income. The 2008 financial crisis was a turning point in the development of this research. Researchers developed the first comprehensive measures of financial resilience. For instance, Lusardi et al. (2011) introduced a measure of emergency preparedness based on the ability to accumulate $2,000 within 30 days. The interest in this topic has further increased due to the effects of the ongoing pandemic. During this period, more sophisticated conceptual frameworks have emerged, including Salignac et al.'s (2019) multidimensional approach and the OECD's (2022) five-component framework.

According to Salignac et al. (2019), financial resilience is a multidimensional construct comprising four interrelated elements: economic resources (e.g., savings and debt), access to financial products and services (e.g., bank accounts), financial knowledge and behavior, and social capital. The OECD framework for financial well-being and resilience, on the other hand, includes the following elements: (a) control over money: day-to-day financial planning and budgeting; (b) managing expenses: timely fulfillment of financial obligations; (c) financial buffer: ability to survive financial shocks; (d) coping with financial stress: managing financial problems without severe negative consequences for mental health, family stability, or long-term financial goals; and (e) financial planning: active saving and setting financial goals.

2.2 Concept of financial resilience in the financial sector

The concept of financial resilience for financial institutions is the result of the combination of two conceptual streams. The first stream is the aforementioned trend derived from the income and budget resilience of households, and the second is the creation of a supervisory framework for financial institutions that could reduce the risk of their collapse and the scale of the impact of defaults on the economy. The origins of the concept of financial resilience of financial institutions date back to the banking crisis of the 1970s, specifically the collapse of Bankhaus Herstatt in Germany in 1974. This event led to the creation of the Basel Committee on Banking Supervision (BCBS) by the governors of the central banks of the G10 countries. At that time, financial resilience was understood as basic solvency and liquidity. The term "financial stability" was used instead of "resilience" (Kheria, 2025). The deregulation of the financial sectors in the 1980s and 1990s fundamentally changed the understanding of financial resilience. During this period, the view developed that financial resilience meant the ability to survive in a competitive market environment. In his work "Nonmonetary Effects of the Financial Crisis ...," Bernanke (1983) laid the theoretical foundation for understanding how disruptions in the financial sector can have real economic effects, influencing the evolution of the concept of resilience.

The introduction of the Basel I regulations in 1988 was an important stage in the development of the concept of resilience. For the first time, an international standard was established that required banks to maintain a minimum capital adequacy ratio of 8%. The key innovation of Basel I was the introduction of a risk-weighting system. For example, government assets were assigned a 0% risk weight; claims on banks incorporated in the OECD were assigned a 20% risk weight; and mortgage loans were assigned a 50%, and commercial loans: 100%. This systematization marked a transition from ad hoc supervisory practices to a systematic, quantitative approach to financial resilience. Capital adequacy, asset quality, liquidity, and profitability were recognized as key determinants of banking sector stability (BCBS, 1988).

Ten years after the implementation of Basel I, work on Basel II (also known as the New Capital Accord) began in 1999. Basel II was published in June 2004 and adopted by the European Union through the Capital Requirements Directive (CRD) Directives 48/2006 and 49/2006. These directives were implemented in individual countries in subsequent years. Basel II aimed to align banks' capital requirements with their actual risk levels and effectively laid the foundation for the modern concept of financial resilience in financial institutions. In particular, Basel II introduced a three-pillar approach:

- Pillar 1: Minimum Capital Requirements
- Pillar 2: Supervisory Review Process
- Pillar 3: Market Discipline – see BCBS (2004).

Importantly, Pillar 1 expanded to include more than just credit risk. It included operational risk and refined the treatment of market risk.

It introduced the concept of operational risk as a separate capital charge linked to events such as losses from fraud, system failures, and legal risks. In terms of credit risk, Basel II allowed for different approaches to risk calculation: The Standardized Approach (using external credit ratings), the Foundation Internal Ratings-Based Approach (F-IRB), and the Advanced Internal Ratings-Based Approach (A-IRB). Pillar 2 gave regulators more authority to review banks' internal risk assessments and require additional capital. Pillar 3 increased disclosure requirements to enhance transparency and enable market participants to evaluate banks' risk profiles (BCBS, 2004). Consequently, Basel II represented an evolution from a simple capital measurement system to a multidimensional assessment of operational capabilities, placing a greater emphasis on internal risk management.

The 2008–2009 financial crisis was an important catalyst for further developing the concept of financial resilience within the financial sector. The crisis revealed the inadequacy of traditional resilience measures. Diamond and Rajan (2009) demonstrated how the fear of asset sell-offs can result in systemic illiquidity, thereby altering the understanding of financial resilience. In the aftermath of the financial crisis, a new framework was developed to strengthen capital and liquidity resilience regulations in the financial sector. Basel III, published in December 2010 and subsequently implemented by 2012, represented a significant reconstruction of financial resilience frameworks. Key changes included the following (BCBS, 2010):

1 Strengthened capital requirements:
   - Minimum Common Equity Tier 1 (CET1): increase from 2% to 4.5% of risk-weighted assets,
   - Tier 1 Capital Ratio: increase from 4% to 6%,
   - Total Capital Ratio: maintained at 8% (changes in quality standards).

2 New capital buffers:
   - Capital Conservation Buffer: +2.5% CET1,
   - Countercyclical Buffer: 0–2.5% (applied during credit booms),
   - G-SIB Surcharge: Additional buffer for systemically important banks.

3 New liquidity ratios:
   - Liquidity Coverage Ratio (LCR): minimum 100% (Tier 1 capital/total exposure, non-risk-based),
   - Net Stable Funding Ratio (NSFR): minimum 100%,
   - Leverage Ratio (Tier 1 Capital/Total Exposure Measure): minimum 3%.

As indicated by the European Central Bank, these measures were aimed at building a more resilient global banking system after the global financial crisis of 2007–2009, which exposed the weaknesses of the previous framework (ECB, 2023b).

The next stage in the development of the concept of financial resilience was creating a comprehensive concept of operational resilience. This term was originally introduced by the British supervisory authorities in such a context; see: BoE, PRA, FCA (2018). The BCBS defined operational resilience as

> The ability of a bank to deliver critical operations through disruption. This ability enables a bank to identify and protect itself from threats and potential failures, respond and adapt to, as well as recover and learn from disruptive events in order to minimise their impact on the delivery of critical operations.
>
> (BCBS, 2021, p. 3)

The BCBS has identified seven key principles for building operational resilience, grouped into the following categories: governance, operational risk management, business continuity planning and testing, mapping interconnections and interdependencies, third-party dependency management, incident management, and Information and Communication Technology, including cybersecurity. This approach integrated into the risk management system, among other things, the identification of critical operations and ensured that banks can continue operations during severe but plausible disruptions (e.g., cyberattacks, pandemics). It strengthened business continuity planning and disaster recovery, including for digital threats.

The final set of BCBS recommendations, known as Basel 3.1 (also called Basel III: Finalizing post-crisis reforms, or Basel III Endgame), was accepted in 2017. Among other changes, Basel 3.1 introduced more granular risk weights and limits on internal models for low-default portfolios with respect to credit risk management. Regarding operational risk, Basel 3.1 introduced the Single Standardized Measurement Approach (SMA). Market risk measures were based on the finalized Fundamental Review of the Trading Book (FRTB), which included stricter capital requirements and the replacement of Market Risk Value-at-Risk (VaR) indicators with Expected Shortfall indicators (BCBS, 2017). Basel 3.1 was originally scheduled to be implemented in January 2023, with a phase-in period ending in 2028. Due mostly to the pandemic, this target has been postponed in many countries. Currently, implementation is planned for 2025 in the United States and 2027 in EU countries. During this period, financial resilience was defined as the ability to survive a crisis and recover quickly. It was also distinguished from the broader concept of financial stability.

The latest stage in the evolution of the concept of financial resilience is linked to the introduction of the Digital Operational Resilience Act (DORA) in January 2025. EU Regulation 2022/2554 establishes unified requirements for the security of networks and information systems. These requirements aim to enable financial institutions to withstand, respond to, and recover from Information and Communication Technology (ICT) disruptions, including cyberattacks and system failures. DORA focuses on five pillars: ICT risk management (governance and organization of ICT risk, identification, protection, detection, response, recovery processes, and backup procedures); ICT-Related Incident Management, Classification, and Reporting (processes for managing and classification ICT incidents and cyber threats, and mandatory reporting); Digital Operational Resilience Testing (regular and advanced testing of ICT systems and tools, including Threat-Led Penetration Testing (TLPT) for critical functions); ICT Third-Party Risk Management and Oversight (managing risks from outsourcing and third-party ICT service providers, including oversight framework for critical third-party providers); and Information Sharing (sharing cyber threat intelligence among financial entities in order to improve collective resilience); see DORA (2025). DORA has therefore introduced requirements for financial institutions to implement a comprehensive ICT risk management framework.

Among other issues that have been developed in recent years in the context of financial resilience, changes in macroprudential policy should also be noted. As indicated by the ECB (2025), there is a shift toward a preventive approach. Already in 17 EEA countries, the Countercyclical Capital Buffer (CCyB) has been activated early to create space for releasing these buffers regardless of the phase of the cycle (so-called positive neutral). This increases the sector's resilience to various shocks, such as a bursting credit market bubble.

In summary, the development of the concept of financial resilience of financial institutions currently encompasses three key dimensions:

1. Financial resilience – capital and liquidity.
2. Operational resilience – continuity of critical business processes, including IT systems.
3. Systemic resilience – functioning under conditions of systemic stress.

2.3 Measurement process and financial resilience indicators

The process of assessing and improving financial resilience can be divided into several stages. The first stage involves determining the applicable regulatory framework that will apply and the scope of measurement. Within this regulatory framework, particular attention should be paid to DORA and the Capital Requirements Regulation (CRR3, 2024), which implemented the final Basel III reforms. Next, key risk areas should be identified, particularly those covering capital and liquidity (including assessment of capital quality (CET1), LCR, and NSFR ratios), operational and ICT risk (including DORA and Financial Conduct Authority (FCA) requirements, such as identifying critical business services and dependencies in the context of both the technology used and the scope of outsourcing), and market and macroeconomic risk (analysis of exposure to economic shocks, interest rates, credit, and market risk). The next step is to establish key metrics such as capital buffers and leverage levels under Basel III, as well as tolerances, for example, in accordance with FCA impact tolerances for critical services.

The next stage should involve resilience testing. Stress testing should cover both macroeconomic scenarios (in accordance with the EU-wide European Banking Authority (EBA) stress test) and operational and cyber risk tests (in accordance with DORA). It is important that the simulations are multidimensional, that is, they take into account both financial and operational risks. After the tests have been carried out, conclusions should be drawn based on their results; that is, an analysis should be conducted and/or remedial actions should be sought. This includes, in particular, the identification of weaknesses in the areas of capital, liquidity, and operational processes. The gap analysis should be followed by the identification and implementation of corrective measures, such as increasing buffers, improving governance rules, and strengthening the resilience of ICT systems to external attacks or failures, including in terms of hardware. The final stage of this process is reporting (including self-assessment and regulatory compliance documentation) and the implementation of continuous improvement practices. Creating a learning organization in this area includes, among other things, updating models and scenarios based on changes in the internal and external environments. Figure 2.1 summarizes the financial resilience measurement process and follow-up actions in financial institutions in the context of European Union countries.

Over the years, a wide range of measures has been developed to measure financial resilience or identify risks. It is worth noting that individual measures are used in different contexts, such as internal management practices, supervisory measures, or regulatory measures (requirements). It is also worth emphasizing that many of these measures are currently being integrated with stress tests to assess ability to absorb losses in various scenarios. At the same time, new types of risks, such as climate, cyber, and geopolitical risks, are being incorporated into the measures and scenarios. One common categorization of indicators is to classify them as:

- Capital and liquidity indicators and buffers,
- Systemic and macroprudential indicators,
- Stress test measures,
- Climate risk and ESG indicators,
- Operational resilience indicators.

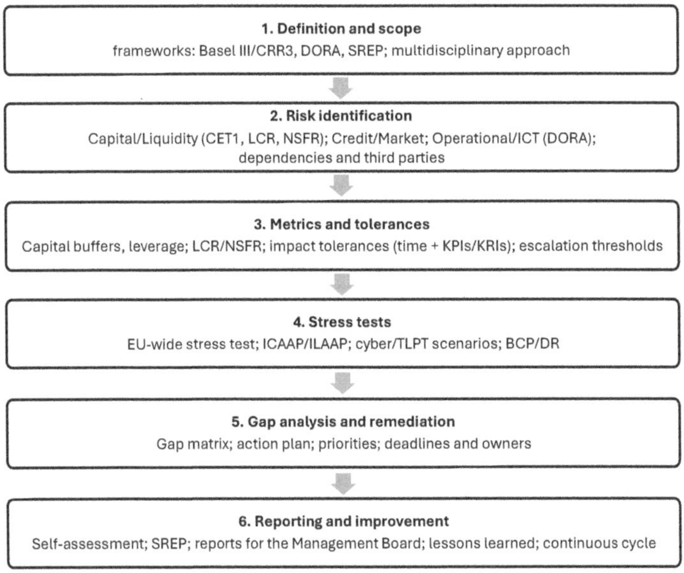

Figure 2.1 Financial resilience framework – process flowchart.

Source: own elaboration based on BCBS, EBA, FCA publications.

Abbreviations: SREP – Supervisory Review and Evaluation Process, CET1 – Common Equity Tier 1 Ratio, LCR – Liquidity Coverage Ratio, NSFR – Net Stable Funding Ratio, KPI – Key Performance Indicator, KRI – Key Risk Indicator, ICAAP – Internal Capital Adequacy Assessment Process, ILAAP – Internal Liquidity Adequacy Assessment Process, TLPT – Threat-Led Penetration Testing, BCP – Business Continuity Plan, DR – Disaster Recovery.

The following capital ratios can be distinguished among the main indicators for capital and liquidity buffers (Basel III/3.1): The CET1 ratio, which is the basic indicator of capital quality; the Total Capital Ratio, which is the total solvency ratio; and the Leverage Ratio, which is the excessive leverage ratio. Capital indicators regarding macroprudential buffers include the countercyclical capital buffer (CCyB), which is activated during a boom and released during a crisis, and the systemic risk buffer (SyRB), which mitigates long-term structural risks. Liquidity indicators primarily include the LCR, which measures the ability to cover outflows over 30 days, and the NSFR, which measures the stability of funding over one year.

Among systemic and strictly macroprudential indicators, the main measures are the Credit-to-GDP gap – a signal of credit risk accumulation, the Non-Performing Loans (NPL) ratio – asset quality, and Systemic Risk Indicators such as SRISK – expected capital shortfall under stress,

CoVaR – conditional risk in the system, and the OFR Contagion Index – vulnerability to the spread of shocks. In addition, the ECB Macroprudential Dashboard has been developed – a set of indicators covering leverage, liquidity, market risk, and real estate.

In the case of stress testing, the main methods of measuring resilience include macroeconomic stress scenarios – the impact of recession, interest rate increases, asset price declines, and idiosyncratic scenarios – for example, cyberattacks and loss of liquidity. Stress tests use outcome measures such as changes in the CET1 ratio in the scenario, capital shortfall (the amount of capital needed to meet requirements), and liquidity gap (the ability to cover outflows).

Another important category of resilience measurement is climate and environmental, social, and governance (ESG) risk, which was mentioned earlier. This category includes indicators such as CRISK (Climate Risk) – expected capital shortfall in a climate stress scenario, Climate Beta – sensitivity of the bank's share price to climate factors, and the Green Asset Ratio – share of green assets in the portfolio.

When measuring operational resilience (in the context of the financial sector), indicators such as Maximum Allowable Outage (MAO) and Recovery Time Objective (RTO) for critical services are used. Cyberattack resilience tests are also used here. It is worth noting that although this is an area of operational resilience, regulators treat it as an element of systemic resilience because operational problems can, among other things, trigger a liquidity crisis. Table 2.1 describes the most popular indicators.

A key element of measuring and managing resilience is defining preferred and undesirable values for individual indicators. These values are presented in Table 2.2 in RAG (Red, Amber, Green) terms:

- Red: Undesirable range, usually requiring an immediate response, such as a remediation plan, strengthening of buffers, or risk reduction.
- Amber: Warning or neutral range, usually requiring enhanced monitoring or preventive measures.
- Green: Desirable range.

These ranges have been determined based on Basel 3.1/CRD V regulatory requirements, EBA/ECB supervisory practices, and academic research findings. Note that the desired values for many of these indicators are institution- or scenario-specific.

It is important to note that the above-listed indicators should be monitored together. Only by combining a set of measures and tools (capital, liquidity, asset quality, the credit cycle, stress tests, systemic connectivity, and non-financial risks) can a complete picture of resilience be obtained.

Table 2.1 Description of the most popular financial resilience indicators

Category	*Metric/indicator*	*What it measures/interpretation*	*Scope*	*Risk type*
Capital Adequacy	Common Equity Tier 1 (CET1) Ratio	Core capital as % of RWA; Loss absorption capacity after regulatory deductions	Micro/Institution	Credit, Market, Operational
Capital Adequacy	Tier 1 Capital Ratio	Core capital plus AT1 as % of RWA; Going-concern capital strength	Micro/Institution	Credit, Market, Operational
Capital Adequacy	Total Capital Ratio	Total regulatory capital as % of RWA; Overall capital adequacy for losses	Micro/Institution	Credit, Market, Operational
Liquidity	Liquidity Coverage Ratio (LCR)	HQLA over net cash outflows (30 days); Short-term liquidity resilience in stress	Micro/Institution	Liquidity
Liquidity	Net Stable Funding Ratio (NSFR)	ASF over RSF; Structural funding stability over 1-year horizon	Micro/Institution	Liquidity, Funding
Asset Quality	Non-Performing Loans (NPL) Ratio	Impaired loans as % of total loans; Credit risk materialization and asset quality	Micro/Institution	Credit
Asset Quality	Loan Loss Provisions Coverage	Provisions as % of NPLs; Forward-looking loss recognition adequacy	Micro/Institution	Credit
Profitability	Return on Assets (ROA)	Net income as % of total assets; Asset utilization efficiency and profitability	Micro/Institution	Credit, Market, Operational
Profitability	Return on Equity (ROE)	Net income as % of shareholders equity; Return to shareholders and capital efficiency	Micro/Institution	Credit, Market, Operational
Profitability	Cost-to-Income Ratio	Operating expenses as % of operating income; Operational efficiency measure	Micro/Institution	Operational
Profitability	Net Interest Margin (NIM)	Net interest income as % of interest-earning assets; Core banking profitability; sensitive to interest rate risk in the banking book (IRRBB) and to the maturity structure of deposits	Micro/Institution	Credit, Market
Systemic Risk	Credit Growth Rate	Annual growth rate of credit to private sector; Credit expansion pace	Macro/Sector/System	Credit, Systemic
Systemic Risk	Credit-to-GDP Gap	Credit-to-GDP deviation from trend; Financial cycle position and systemic risk	Macro/System	Systemic, Cyclical

Systemic Risk	Debt Service Ratio (DSR)	Debt service payments (capital and interest) as % of income; Borrower repayment capacity stress	Macro/Sector	Credit, Macro
Operational/ Management Risk	Loan-to-Deposit Ratio	Total loans as % of deposits; Funding structure and liquidity transformation	Micro/Institution	Liquidity, Credit
Operational/ Management Risk	Large Exposure Ratio	Large exposures as % of Tier 1 capital; Concentration risk exposure	Micro/Institution	Concentration
Operational/ Management Risk	Leverage Ratio	Tier 1 capital as % of total exposure (on- and off-balance); Simple leverage constraint	Micro/Institution	General
Operational/ Management Risk	Z-Score	Typically: (ROA + Equity/Assets)/ROA volatility; Bank stability and insolvency distance	Micro/Institution	Insolvency, Systemic
Operational/ Management Risk	Stress Test Capital Depletion	Capital depletion under adverse scenario; Forward-looking capital adequacy	Micro/System	Credit, Market, Operational
Operational/ Management Risk	Operational Risk Capital	Capital requirement for operational risk; Op. risk loss absorption capacity; based on SMA (Business Indicator + Internal Loss Multiplier)	Micro/Institution	Operational
Operational/ Management Risk	Expected Shortfall	Expected Shortfall with liquidity horizons; market capital measure according to FRTB	Micro/Institution	Market
Macroprudential	Countercyclical Capital Buffer	Additional capital buffer (0–2.5% CET1); Cyclical systemic risk mitigation; Based on loan/GDP gap	Macro/System	Systemic, Cyclical
Macroprudential	Systemic Risk Buffer	Address long-term, non-cyclical systemic or structural risks; may be imposed on the entire sector or subsets of exposures	Macro/System	Systemic
Macroprudential	Asset Quality Index	Weighted average of asset quality indicators; Composite credit risk measure	Micro/Sector	Credit
Macroprudential	Fair Value Margin (FVM)	Fair value assets minus book liabilities over equity; Market-based resilience; Alternatives: price-to-book, market leverage, distance-to-default (Merton)	Micro/Institution	Credit, Market, Liquidity
Macroprudential	Financial Fragility Index	Composite index of financial stress indicators; System-wide fragility measure; Numerous variants exist	Macro/System	Systemic

Source: own elaboration, based on the references presented in Table 2.2.

Table 2.2 Metrics and RAG thresholds for the most popular financial resilience indicators

Metric/indicator	*Unit/threshold*	*RAG thresholds (illustrative)*	*Key references (literature/regulatory sources)*
Common Equity Tier 1 (CET1) Ratio	% (≥4.5% + combined buffers; plus any P2R/P2G as applicable)	Green: >10.5%, Amber: 7–10.5%, Red: <7%	BCBS (2017); Acharya et al. (2014); Drehmann and Juselius (2014)
Tier 1 Capital Ratio	% (≥6.0%)	Green: >8.5%, Amber: 6.5–8.5%, Red: <6.5%	BCBS (2017); Admati and Hellwig (2013); ECB (2023a)
Total Capital Ratio	% (≥8.0%)	Green: >12%, Amber: 8.5–12%, Red: <8.5%	BCBS (2017); Hanson et al. (2011); EBA Guidelines (2020)
Liquidity Coverage Ratio (LCR)	% (≥100%)	Green: >130%, Amber: 100–130%, Red: <100%	BCBS (2013); Banerjee and Mio (2018); ECB (2013)
Net Stable Funding Ratio (NSFR)	% (≥100%)	Green: >120%, Amber: 100–120%, Red: <100%	BCBS (2014); King (2013); EBA Guidelines on NSFR (2021b)
Non-Performing Loans (NPL) Ratio	% (Institution-specific)	Green: <3%, Amber: 3–5%, Red: >5%	EBA Risk Dashboard; Beck et al. (2015); Espinoza and Prasad (2010)
Loan Loss Provisions Coverage	% (≥70% good practice)	Green: >80%, Amber: 50–80%, Red: <50%	IFRS 9 (2018); Beatty and Liao (2011); ECB (2024)
Return on Assets (ROA)	% (0.5–1.5% typical)	Green: >1%, Amber: 0.4–1%, Red: <0.4%	Demirgüç-Kunt and Huizinga (1999); Beck et al. (2013); EBA Risk Dashboard
Return on Equity (ROE)	% (8–15% typical)	Green: >12%, Amber: 8–12%, Red: <8%	Demirgüç-Kunt and Huizinga (2010)
Cost-to-Income Ratio	% (<60% efficient)	Green: <50%, Amber: 50–65%, Red: >65%	Williams (2004)
Net Interest Margin (NIM)	% (2–4% typical)	Green: >2.5%, Amber: 1.5–2.5%, Red: <1.5%	Demirgüç-Kunt and Huizinga (1999); Claessens et al. (2018)
Credit Growth Rate	% (GDP- and inflation-adjusted where possible)	Green: –2% to +8%, Amber: –% to –2% and 8%–15%, Red: < –5% or > 15%	Schularick and Taylor (2012); Jordà et al. (2015)
Credit-to-GDP Gap	pp deviation from long-term trend; positive values signal build-up	Green: |gap| ≤ 2pp, Amber: 2–10pp or –5 to –2pp, Red: >10pp or < –5pp	Drehmann and Tsatsaronis (2014); Borio and Lowe (2002); EBA Risk Dashboard

Debt Service Ratio (DSR)	% Of income (≤40% sustainable)	Green: <25%, Amber: 25–40%, Red: >40%	Drehmann and Juselius (2014); BCBS (2013); Lombardi et al. (2017)
Loan-to-Deposit Ratio	% (prudent range ~80–100%; business-model dependent)	Green: 80–100%, Amber: 70–80% or 100–110%, Red: <70% or >110%	Berger and Bouwman (2009); DeYoung and Jang (2016);
Large Exposure Ratio	% (≤25% of Tier 1 capital to a single client/group)	Green: <15%, Amber: 15–25%, Red: >25%	BCBS (2014)
Leverage Ratio	% (Tier 1 capital/total exposure; ≥3% regulatory minimum)	Green: >4%, Amber: 3–4%, Red: <3%	BCBS (2014); Blum (2008); ECB (2021b)
Z-Score	Dimensionless (higher = more stable); Z = (ROA + Equity/Assets)/σ(ROA)	Green: ≥ 66th percentile vs peers/history, Amber: 33–66th percentile, Red: <33rd percentile	Laeven and Levine (2009); Beck et al. (2013)
Stress Test Capital Depletion	pp change in CET1 (or total capital) under adverse scenario	Green: <2pp, Amber: 2–5pp, Red: >5pp	EBA (2025) Stress Tests
Operational Risk Capital	% Of total RWAs (OpRisk RWA share under SMA); no hard regulatory threshold	Green: <8%, Amber: 8–15%, Red: >15%	BCBS (2017); Chernobai et al. (2011)
Expected Shortfall	Regulatory market risk measure: ES(97.5% confidence level) with liquidity horizons; monitored as Market Risk RWA/Total RWA	Green: <5%, Amber: 5–10%, Red: >10%	BCBS (2019), EBA (2021a)
Countercyclical Capital Buffer	% (0–2.5% CET1 depending on cycle)	Green: 0–1%, Amber: 1–2%, Red: >2%	BCBS (2010); Drehmann et al. (2010); ESRB (2014)
Systemic Risk Buffer	% Typically expressed as an additional CET1 buffer (1–3%)	Green: 0–1.5%, Amber: 1.5–3%, Red: >3%	BCBS (2022)
Asset Quality Index	Index (0–100; higher = better asset quality)	Green: ≥60, Amber: 40–60, Red: <40	Betz et al. (2014); Poghosyan (2013); IMF Financial Soundness Indicators
Fair Value Margin (FVM)	Ratio (>0 indicates positive cushion; custom methodologies)	Green: >0.30, Amber: 0.10–0.30, Red: <0.10	Barth and Landsman (2010); Cantrell et al. (2014)
Financial Fragility Index	Index (0–1, <0.3 stable); method-dependent	Green: <0.2, Amber: 0.2–0.4, Red: >0.4	Nelson and Perli (2007); Cheang and Choy (2011); Illing and Liu (2006)

Source: own elaboration.

2.4 Directions for further research

The concept of financial resilience is constantly evolving due to changes in the environment, particularly with regard to technology, growing economic interdependencies, increasing climate risks, and regular severe shocks to the financial system. Prospective research directions and the evolution of financial resilience include multi-dimensional climate-digital-financial adaptation.

Climate-related financial risks, in particular, have been an emerging area of research in financial resilience for several years. This research intensified at the beginning of the current decade under the strong leadership of the ECB. The ECB is conducting "quantitative work aimed at capturing climate-related risks to financial stability. This includes estimating financial system exposures to climate-related risks, upgrading banking sector scenario analysis and monitoring developments in the financing of the green transition." (ECB, 2021a, p. 100).

Key findings include the following: (IMF, 2024)

- Bank exposures to climate risks, such as physical risks (e.g., floods and hurricanes) and transition risk drivers (e.g., regulatory changes and decarbonization), are not evenly distributed. Consequently, supervisors must require banks to map climate risk concentrations and incorporate them into stress tests.
- There is a "prevalence of exposures amongst more vulnerable banks" in certain regions; that is, banks in some jurisdictions (e.g., emerging markets, regions with high exposure to climate change) have a higher share of risky assets on their balance sheets.
- There is a strong "inter-temporal dependency conditioning the interaction of transition and physical risks," meaning physical and transition risks are linked over time. Consequently, risk models must consider dynamic scenarios and time dependencies, not just static assessments. Their development requires advanced analytical tools and artificial intelligence (AI).

In the context of climate risk and bank resilience, it is also worth noting the 2025 revision of the CRISK index (Jung et al., 2025), which measures the expected capital shortfall of a bank under climate stress (transition risk). Recently, sectoral guidelines developed by the UN Environment Programme Finance Initiative (UNEP FI, 2025) on embedding adaptation and resilience in banking practices and linking them to public policies contained in national adaptation plans (NAPs) have also been published.

Another important theme in research and concept evolution is AI-enhanced resilience. AI emerges as a key enabler of financial resilience. AI can reduce response times to security incidents by more than 85%

(Kumar, 2025), and machine learning systems achieve 90%–95% effectiveness in detecting cybersecurity threats (Ahsan et al., 2022). Dr. Dimitrios Salampasis points out that AI "emerges as an epistemic shift in how financial institutions comprehend, predict, and adapt within an environment driven not only by risk but also by ambiguity (ambiguity is the new norm)" (Salampasis, 2025).

Future directions also include integrating emerging technologies into financial resilience research. The NTT Data Banking Trends 2025 report identifies the following issues here (NTT, 2025):

- Central Bank Digital Currencies, which, among other things, increase the financial system's dependence on digital infrastructure and real-time payment systems,
- Embedded finance, which involves embedding financial services (e.g., loans and payments) into non-financial applications and platforms (e.g., e-commerce and ERP), creating new operational risks and increasing the complexity of the system,
- The mainstreaming trend of AI integration as a core component of banking operations, which enables automation, predictive analytics, and personalized customer experiences,
- Subscription-based banking models, where new risk indicators emerge: churn rate, lifetime value, and not just classic credit indicators. Consequently, reputation risk management is a key challenge.

In summary of this chapter, it is worth noting the need for multi-disciplinary approaches in the field of financial resilience (Pacelli, 2025). The future development of this concept requires deepening of the integration of a number of perspectives in order to holistically cover systematically evolving operational risks in particular. Perspectives to be methodically considered include:

- Economics – macro-financial linkages and systemic risk propagation.
- Behavioral sciences – human factors in operational resilience.
- Climate science – physical risk modeling and scenario development.
- Computer science – advanced AI/machine language (ML) applications in risk management.

References

Acharya, V. V., Engle, R., & Pierret, D. (2014). Testing macroprudential stress tests: The risk of regulatory risk weights. *Journal of Monetary Economics*, *65*, 36–53. https://doi.org/10.1016/j.jmoneco.2014.04.002

Admati, A. R., & Hellwig, M. F. (2013). *The bankers' new clothes: What's wrong with banking and what to do about it*. Princeton University Press.

Ahsan, M., Nygard, K. E., Gomes, R., Chowdhury, M. M., Rifat, N., & Connolly, J. F. (2022). Cybersecurity threats and their mitigation approaches using machine learning—A review. *Journal of Cybersecurity and Privacy*, *2*(3), 527–555.

Banerjee, R. N., & Mio, H. (2018). The impact of liquidity regulation on banks. *Journal of Financial Intermediation*, *35*, 30–44. https://doi.org/10.1016/j.jfi.2017.05.008

Barth, M. E., & Landsman, W. R. (2010). How did financial reporting contribute to the financial crisis? *European Accounting Review*, *19*(3), 399–423. https://doi.org/10.1080/09638180.2010.498619

BCBS (1988). *International convergence of capital measurement and capital standards*. Basel Committee on Banking Supervision, Bank for International Settlements, July 1988.

BCBS (2004). *International convergence of capital measurement and capital standards. A revised framework*. Basel Committee on Banking Supervision, Bank for International Settlements, June 2024.

BCBS (2010). *Basel III: A global regulatory framework for more resilient banks and banking systems*. Basel Committee on Banking Supervision, Bank for International Settlements, December 2010, revised June 2011.

BCBS (2013). *Basel III: The liquidity coverage ratio and liquidity risk monitoring tools*. Bank for International Settlements. https://www.bis.org/publ/bcbs238.htm

BCBS (2014). *Basel III: The net stable funding ratio*. Basel Committee on Banking Supervision, Bank for International Settlements, October.

BCBS (2017). Basel III: Finalizing post-crisis reforms. Basel Committee on Banking Supervision, Bank for International Settlements, December 2017.

BCBS (2019). *Minimum capital requirements for market risk*. Basel Committee on Banking Supervision, Bank for International Settlements, published in January 2019 (rev. February 2019).

BCBS (2021). *Principles for operational resilience*. Basel Committee on Banking Supervision, Bank for International Settlements, published in March.

BCBS (2022). *Buffer usability and cyclicality in the Basel framework*. Basel Committee on Banking Supervision, Bank for International Settlements, published in October.

Beatty, A., & Liao, S. (2011). Do delays in expected loss recognition affect banks' willingness to lend? *Journal of Accounting and Economics*, *52*(1), 1–20. https://doi.org/10.1016/j.jacceco.2011.02.002

Beck, T., Demirgüç-Kunt, A., & Merrouche, O. (2013). Islamic vs. conventional banking: Business model, efficiency and stability. *Journal of Banking & Finance*, *37*(2), 433–447. https://doi.org/10.1016/j.jbankfin.2012.09.016

Beck, T., Jakubik, P., & Piloiu, A. (2015). *Non-performing loans: What matters in addition to the economic cycle?* European Central Bank Working Paper Series, No. 1836.

Berger, A. N., & Bouwman, C. H. S. (2009). Bank liquidity creation. *Review of Financial Studies*, *22*(9), 3779–3837. https://doi.org/10.1093/rfs/hhn104

Bernanke, B. S. (1983). *Non-monetary effects of the financial crisis in the propagation of the Great Depression*. National Bureau of Economic Research, No. w1054.

Betz, F., Oprică, S., Peltonen, T. A., & Sarlin, P. (2014). Predicting distress in European banks. *Journal of Banking & Finance*, *45*, 225–241. https://doi.org/10.1016/j.jbankfin.2013.11.041

Blum, J. M. (2008). Why 'Basel II' may need a leverage ratio restriction. *Journal of Banking & Finance*, *32*(8), 1699–1707.

BoE, PRA, FCA (2018). *Building the UK financial sector's operational resilience*. Bank of England DP01/18, Prudential Regulation Authority (PRA) DP01/18, Financial Conduct Authority (FCA) DP18/04.

Borio, C., & Lowe, P. (2002). Assessing the risk of banking crises. *BIS Quarterly Review*, December, 43–54.

Cantrell, B. W., McInnis, J. M., & Yust, C. G. (2014). Predicting credit losses: Loan fair values versus historical costs. *The Accounting Review*, *89*(1), 147–176. https://doi.org/10.2308/accr-50586

Carroll, C. (1997). Buffer-stock saving and the life-cycle/permanent income hypothesis. *Quarterly Journal of Economics*, *112*(1), 1–55.

Cheang, N., & Choy, I. (2011). Aggregate financial stability index for an early warning system. *Macao Monetary Research Bulletin*, *21*(1), 27–51.

Chernobai, A., Jorion, P., & Yu, F. (2011). The determinants of operational risk in U.S. financial institutions. *Journal of Financial and Quantitative Analysis*, *46*(6), 1683–1725. https://doi.org/10.1017/S0022109011000500

Claessens, S., Coleman, N., & Donnelly, M. (2018). "Low-for-long" interest rates and banks' interest margins and profitability: Cross-country evidence. *Journal of Financial Intermediation*, *35*, 1–16. https://doi.org/10.1016/j.jfi.2017.05.004

CRR3 (2024). Regulation (EU) 2024/1623 of the European Parliament and of the Council of May 31, 2024 amending Regulation (EU) No 575/2013 as regards requirements for credit risk, credit valuation adjustment risk, operational risk, market risk and the output floor.

Demirgüç-Kunt, A., & Huizinga, H. (1999). Determinants of commercial bank interest margins and profitability: Some international evidence. *World Bank Economic Review*, *13*(2), 379–408. https://doi.org/10.1093/wber/13.2.379

Demirgüç-Kunt, A., & Huizinga, H. (2010). Bank activity and funding strategies: The impact on risk and returns. *Journal of Financial Economics*, *98*(3), 626–650. https://doi.org/10.1016/j.jfineco.2010.06.004

DeYoung, R., & Jang, K. Y. (2016). Do banks actively manage their liquidity? *Journal of Banking & Finance*, *66*, 143–161. https://doi.org/10.1016/j.jbankfin.2015.11.013

Diamond, D. W., & Rajan, R. G. (2009). *Fear of fire sales and the credit freeze*. National Bureau of Economic Research, No. w14925.

DORA (2025). "Regulation (EU) 2022/2554 of the European Parliament and of the Council of 14 December 2022 on digital operational resilience for the financial sector".

Drehmann, M., Borio, C., Gambacorta, L., Jiménez, G., & Trucharte, C. (2010). *Countercyclical capital buffers: Exploring options*. BIS Working Papers No. 317. https://www.bis.org/publ/work317.htm

Drehmann, M., & Juselius, M. (2014). Evaluating early warning indicators of banking crises: Satisfying policy requirements. *International Journal of Forecasting*, *30*(3), 759–780. https://doi.org/10.1016/j.ijforecast.2013.10.002

Drehmann, M., & Tsatsaronis, K. (2014). The credit-to-GDP gap and countercyclical capital buffers: Questions and answers. *BIS Quarterly Review*, March, 55–73. https://www.bis.org/publ/qtrpdf/r_qt1403g.pdf

EBA (2020). *EBA guidelines on loan origination and monitoring*. European Banking Authority. https://www.eba.europa.eu

EBA (2021a) *Guidelines on criteria for the use of data inputs in the risk-measurement model referred to in Article 325bc of Regulation (EU) No 575/2013 (Capital Requirements Regulation)*. European Banking Authority, EBA/GL/2021/07.

EBA (2021b). *Guidelines on the net stable funding ratio (NSFR)*. European Banking Authority. https://www.eba.europa.eu

EBA (2025). *Stress test 2025*. European Banking Authority. https://www.eba.europa.eu/risk-and-data-analysis/risk-analysis/eu-wide-stress-testing

EBA Risk dashboard. *European banking authority*. https://www.eba.europa.eu/risk-and-data-analysis/risk-analysis/risk-monitoring/risk-dashboard

ECB. (2013). Regulation (EU) No 575/2013 on prudential requirements for credit institutions and investment firms. *Official Journal of the European Union, L176*, 1–337. https://eur-lex.europa.eu/eli/reg/2013/575/oj

ECB (2021a). *ECB financial stability review (May 2021)*. European Central Bank.

ECB (2021b). *ECB annual report on supervisory activities 2020*. European Central Bank https://www.bankingsupervision.europa.eu

ECB (2023a). *ECB financial stability review (November 2023)*. European Central Bank.

ECB (2023b). *Macroprudential Bulletin 23*. European Central Bank, December 2023.

ECB (2024). *IFRS 9 overlays and model improvements for novel risks. Identifying best practices for capturing novel risks in loan loss provisions*. European Central Bank, July 2024.

ECB (2025). *Macroprudential bulletin 31*. European Central Bank, August 2025.

Espinoza, R., & Prasad, A. (2010). *Nonperforming loans in the GCC banking system and their macroeconomic effects*. International Monetary Fund. Retrieved from https://www.scirp.org/reference/referencespapers?referenceid=3379048

ESRB (2014). *Recommendation of the European Systemic Risk Board of 18 June 2014 on guidance for setting countercyclical buffer rates*. European Systemic Risk Board, 2014/C 293/01.

Hanson, S. G., Kashyap, A. K., & Stein, J. C. (2011). A macroprudential approach to financial regulation. *Journal of Economic Perspectives*, *25*(1), 3–28. https://doi.org/10.1257/jep.25.1.3

Holling, C. S. (1973). Resilience and stability of ecological systems. *Annual Review of Ecology and Systematics*, *4*, 1–23. https://doi.org/10.1146/annurev.es.04.110173.000245

IFRS. (2018). *IFRS 9 financial instruments*. International Financial Reporting Standards. https://www.ifrs.org

Illing, M., & Liu, Y. (2006). Measuring financial stress in a developed country: An application to Canada. *Journal of Financial Stability*, *2*(3), 243–265. https://doi.org/10.1016/j.jfs.2006.06.002

IMF (2023a). *IMF annual report 2023*. International Monetary Fund

IMF (2023b). *Macroprudential policies and capital controls over financial cycles*. International Monetary Fund, WP/23/171.

IMF (2024). *2024 revised basel core principles for effective banking supervision*. International Monetary Fund, July 12, 2024.

IMF. *Financial soundness indicators*. IMF Data. https://legacydata.imf.org/?sk=51b096fa-2cd2-40c2-8d09-0699cc1764da

Jordà, Ò., Schularick, M., & Taylor, A. M. (2015). Leveraged bubbles. *Journal of Monetary Economics*, *76*, S1–S20. https://doi.org/10.1016/j.jmoneco.2014.10.002

Jung, H., Engle, R. F., & Berner, R. (2025). CRISK: measuring the climate risk exposure of the financial system. *Journal of Financial Economics*, *171*, 104076.

Kheria, A. (2025). The evolution of basel regulations. Retrieved from https://www.linkedin.com/pulse/evolution-basel-regulations-ankit-kheria-lrdqf, accessed on 25.09.2025

King, M. (2013). The Basel III net stable funding ratio and bank net interest margins. *Journal of Banking & Finance*, *37*(11), 4144–4156. https://doi.org/10.1016/j.jbankfin.2013.07.017

Kumar, S. (2025). Automated cybersecurity incident response: How AI reduces response time by 85%. *CyberTech Journals*, July 28, 2025. Retrieved from https://cybertechjournals.com/automated-cybersecurity-incident-response/, accessed on 21.09.2025

Laeven, L., & Levine, R. (2009). Bank governance, regulation and risk taking. *Journal of Financial Economics*, *93*(2), 259–275. https://doi.org/10.1016/j.jfineco.2008.09.003

Leland, H. E. (1968). Saving and uncertainty: The precautionary demand for saving. *The Quarterly Journal of Economics*, Vol. 82, No. 3, 465–473.

Lombardi, M. J., Mohanty, M. S., & Shim, I. (2017). The real effects of household debt in the short and long run. BIS Working Papers No. 607.

Lusardi, A., Schneider, D. J., & Tufano, P. (2011). *Financially fragile households: Evidence and implications*. National Bureau of Economic Research, No. w17072.

Modigliani, F., & Brumberg, R. H. (1954). Utility analysis and the consumption function: An interpretation of cross-section data. In K. K. Kurihara (Ed.), *Post-Keynesian economics* (pp. 388–436). New Brunswick, NJ: Rutgers University Press.

Nelson, W. R., & Perli, R. (2007). Selected indicators of financial stability. *Risk Measurement and Systemic Risk*, *4*, 343–372.

NTT (2025). *Banking trends 2025*. NTT Data Inc. Report.

OECD (2022). *OECD/INFE toolkit for measuring financial literacy and financial inclusion 2022*. OECD Publishing, Paris. https://doi.org/10.1787/cbc4114f-en.

Pacelli, V. (2025). *Systemic risk and complex networks in modern financial systems* (p. 412). Springer Nature.

Poghosyan, T. (2013). Financial intermediation costs in low income countries: The role of regulatory, institutional, and macroeconomic factors. *Economic Systems*, *37*(1), 92–110.

Salampasis, D. (2025). Unleashing AI's potential in financial resilience: Insights from Dr Dimitrios Salampasis. *Financial Services Institute of Australasia (FINSIA)*. Retrieved from https://finsia.com/news-and-resources/unleashing-ais-potential-in-financial-resilience-insights-from-dr-dimitrios-salampasis-f-fin , accessed on 21.09.2025

Salignac, F., Marjolin, A., Reeve, R., & Muir, K. (2019). Conceptualizing and measuring financial resilience: A multidimensional framework. *Social Indicators Research*, *145*, 17–38.

Sandmo, A. (1970). The effect of uncertainty on saving decisions. *The Review of Economic Studies*, Vol. 37, Issue 3, 353–360.

Schularick, M., & Taylor, A. M. (2012). Credit booms gone bust: Monetary policy, leverage cycles, and financial crises, 1870–2008. *American Economic Review*, *102*(2), 1029–1061. https://doi.org/10.1257/aer.102.2.1029

Tahir, M. S., & Richards, D. W. (2025). A systematic literature review of financial resilience: antecedents, consequences and future research agenda. *Journal of Financial Regulation and Compliance*, *33*(4), 592–615.

UNEP FI (2025). *Practical guidance on implementing adaptation and resilience for banks*. UN Environment Programme Finance Initiative, July 2025.

Williams, J. (2004). Determining management behavior in European banking. *Journal of Banking & Finance*, *28*(10), 2427–2460. https://doi.org/10.1016/j.jbankfin.2003.09.010

3 Financial resilience of financial institutions

Ewa Kulińska-Sadłocha

3.1 Introduction

The resilience of financial institutions, or of the financial system as a whole, is the capability to perform core functions in the economy in a sustained and effective manner despite unexpected disruptions and dynamically changing conditions (NEF, 2015). It is a dynamic concept that comprises not only loss absorption but also adaptation and the transformation of operating models in response to new challenges (Duchek, 2020). Financial system resilience ensures that households can access funds, firms can finance investment, and governments can fund essential services—even during crises (Soliwoda, 2020). Experiences of recent decades—the 2007–2009 global financial crisis, the euro-area sovereign debt crisis, the COVID-19 pandemic, armed conflicts, and climate-related phenomena—have exposed the limits of traditional operating models and the need for a systemic approach to resilience that connects financial fundamentals with operational resilience, organisational culture, reputation, and the integration of Environmental, Social, and Governance (ESG) factors (KPMG, 2020).

Today's financial-market participants operate amid high uncertainty: shifting macroeconomic parameters, accelerated digitalisation, climate transition, global capital flows, and population ageing. At the same time, strong interconnections among sector participants (banks, insurers, funds, and capital markets) and the growing importance of non-bank entities and fintechs increase vulnerability to shocks, while local problems can quickly escalate to the systemic level (IMF, 2025). Non-financial factors (environmental, climate, social, and geopolitical) are gaining in importance, and their transmission channels often lie beyond the direct control of institutions, supervisors, and governments (Kulińska-Sadłocha, 2024).

The aim of the chapter is to identify and systematise the key determinants of financial resilience at both the institutional and system-wide levels, with particular emphasis on the role of regulation, supervision, and tools supporting such resilience. The analysis focuses

DOI: 10.4324/9781003648840-3

on the European perspective, in which building the resilience of financial institutions is closely linked to the pursuit of sustainable development goals such as financial inclusion, climate transition, innovation, and strengthening stable institutions and partnerships. In this context, the European Green Deal (EC, 2019) and the Strategy for Financing the Transition to a Sustainable Economy (EC, 2021) set the framework for integrating financial resilience with the EU's climate and economic transformation agenda.

3.2 Financial system stability and resilience

Financial system stability is most commonly defined as a state in which the financial system performs its core functions in the economy (capital allocation and distribution, payment intermediation, and risk management) on a continuous basis, even when unexpected and severe disturbances occur (Dobrzańska et al., 2017). A stable system both absorbs shocks and limits their transmission to the real economy, ensuring access to finance for firms and households and enabling the state to conduct effective economic policy (including policies supporting the energy-climate transition and financial inclusion) (Cipollone, 2025).

Crisis experience points to the financial system's susceptibility to domino effects. Disruptions in one institution can quickly spread across the sector, triggering panic, liquidity crises, and a fall in public confidence (FSF, 2008). Conversely, the materialisation of risks in the real sector (e.g., excessive household indebtedness or the default of large entities) can destabilise the financial sector, especially banks (Zioło et al., 2021). The stability of an individual financial institution means the ability to maintain balance and return to normal functioning after a shock. It is the foundation for further development of the institution or the system and is an important element of financial resilience—a broader and more dynamic concept than stability. Resilience means not only maintaining functions during disturbances but also rapidly adapting to new conditions and transforming the mode of operation in response to long-term trends (Daadmehr, 2024). It thus goes beyond stability, encompassing flexibility, innovation, and building of long-term advantage (Figure 3.1).

The literature distinguishes three complementary dimensions of resilience (Colloff et al., 2017; Jeans et al., 2017; Martens, 2023):

- Absorption of shocks—the ability to survive and maintain functions, that is, to absorb losses, maintain liquidity, and limit risk transmission to financial-market participants; the aim is to cushion crisis effects, with capital and liquidity buffers, asset quality, reserves, and contingency mechanisms as the foundation.

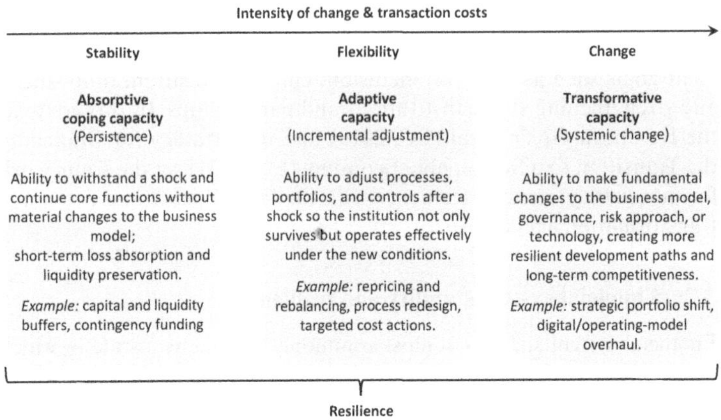

Figure 3.1 Elements of resilience of financial institutions.

Source: own elaboration based on Tanner et al., 2017.

- Adaptation—the capability to adjust quickly to new post-crisis conditions, rebuild capital, and regain the confidence of clients and investors; this includes, inter alia, strategy modification, portfolio restructuring, and operational adjustments to the new environment; the aim is recovery and business continuity (Mullan, 2022).
- Transformation—a lasting change in the rules of operation, infrastructure, and capital allocation that goes beyond absorptive and adaptive capacities; it is long term in nature and leads to a fundamental overhaul of the business model, creating a new institutional order and strengthening innovation.

Taken together, these three elements provide a full picture of resilience in financial institutions: from short-term loss absorption, through medium-term adjustment to new conditions, to the introduction of structural changes that enhance the long-term stability and competitiveness of institutions and the entire system (including through the development of sustainable business models) (Olsson et al., 2016).

An integral component of stability and a central pillar of resilience is operational resilience, which encompasses, among others, business continuity management, risk management (including third-party and cybersecurity risks), as well as facilities management. A failure of payment systems, a cyberattack, or a breakdown of market infrastructure can paralyse the system regardless of sound financial health (Benoit Dupont, 2019; ESMA, 2025). Institutions that invest in innovation, business-model transformation, and the development of risk-management capabilities respond more quickly to regulatory, technological, or demographic change, thereby increasing their resilience (NEF, 2015). As a result, they become stabilisers of the economy, sustaining public trust and ensuring an uninterrupted flow of financing to the real sector even in times of high uncertainty (Atkins et al., 2024). Resilience therefore has systemic, institutional, and social dimensions. It is not merely a matter of financial-system safety but directly translates into societal well-being and long-term socio-economic development (Cipollone, 2025).

3.3 Determinants of the financial resilience of financial institutions

Resilience is shaped by a wide spectrum of internal (financial and non-financial) factors that institutions can manage and external (systemic) factors that lie outside their direct control yet are material for their risk profile (Table 3.1).

Table 3.1 Determinants of financial institutions' resilience (synthetic view)

Factors	*Characteristics and significance for resilience*
Financial	Capital (capital adequacy), liquidity (LCR, NSFR, contingency funding), asset quality (NPLs, IFRS 9), and diversification of income sources. These are the primary sources of loss absorption and liquidity maintenance. Key for banks (CRD/CRR), insurers (Solvency II), and pension funds (coverage of liabilities). A foundation of central bank credibility in monetary policy.
Organisational	Quality of management and corporate governance, risk culture, RAF, effectiveness of internal audit and controls, consistency of strategy with transition plans. They determine the institution's ability to take proper decisions in a crisis and support the stability of critical services in banking, insurance, and payment firms.
Operational	Business continuity (BCP/DRP), cybersecurity, third-party risk management (outsourcing, cloud, SLAs), DORA requirements. A prerequisite for uninterrupted delivery of critical services (payments, settlement, insurance, pension funds). For a central bank—ensuring the robustness of payment systems; for fintechs and payment firms—a key dimension of stability. Strong digital resilience reduces the risk of operational paralysis and run-like dynamics in mobile channels.
Strategic/ESG	Integration of climate and ESG risks into Enterprise Risk Management (ERM), compliance with regulations (CSRD, SFDR, TCFD, EU Taxonomy, NGFS). Building sustainable business models facilitates access to finance and lowers the cost of capital (banks, investment funds); increases insurers' resilience to climate risk (reinsurance, catastrophe loss models); supports reputation and competitiveness; and integrates data and credible disclosures to curb greenwashing and strengthen sector-wide resilience.

(*Continued*)

Table 3.1 (Continued)

Factors	*Characteristics and significance for resilience*
Reputational	Transparency, ethics, reliable disclosures, and rapid crisis communication. They limit the risk of bank runs, mass policy cancellations, or fund withdrawals; for a central bank—sustain trust in the currency and monetary policy; for payment firms—build customer trust in transaction security.
Geopolitical	Wars, sanctions, trade tensions, geo-economic fragmentation, supply-chain disruption. They affect asset valuations and banks' funding costs; increase catastrophe risk for insurers; undermine confidence in investment funds; require stabilisation actions from central banks and governments (swap lines, interventions). They reinforce the need for currency and geographic portfolio diversification.
Technological	Cyberattacks, system failures, outsourcing, and cloud risks; run risk in stablecoins, tokenisation, and DLT risks. For banks and payment firms—critical threats to the continuity of payments and settlement; for funds—operational disruption risk; for the central bank—a challenge to monetary stability and payment systems. It requires intensive SupTech/RegTech monitoring.
Environmental & climate	Extreme weather events, energy transition, and stranded-asset risk. They burden insurers' balance sheets (rising claims); for banks—impact credit-portfolio quality (especially energy and real estate); for funds—risk of loss in high-emission assets. They affect collateral valuations and LTV ratios.
Social & demographic	Demographic change, digitalisation of services, rising customer expectations, and energy poverty. They shape banks' and payment firms' business models (service digitalisation); determine pension funds' long-term liabilities; affect insurance markets (e.g., growing demand for health and retirement products). They require inclusive products and operationally resilient digital channels.
Macroeconomic & market	Business cycle, interest-rate swings, asset-price corrections, and real-estate downturns. They determine banks' income-generation capacity and credit-portfolio quality; affect the profitability of investment and pension funds; for the central bank—shape the monetary-policy framework. They determine buffer needs and stress-test scenarios.
Sectoral (NBFI)	The growing role of hedge funds, private credit, and other NBFIs with leverage and liquidity mismatches. They can amplify systemic contagion risk, especially through links with banks; for funds—necessitate anti-run mechanisms (swing pricing, redemption gates); for regulators and central banks—a key area of macroprudential oversight.
Client-related (behavioural)	Panic, bank runs, mass deposit withdrawals, liquidation of investments and policies, and concentration of uninsured deposits. Critical for banks (deposit-run risk); for investment funds—mass redemption risk; for insurers—policy lapse risk; for payment firms—threat to trust in payment infrastructure. Requires precise communication playbooks and concentration limits.

Source: own elaboration based on NEF, 2015; BIS, 2016; KPMG, 2019; Chortareas, 2023.

Early assessments of stability and resilience focused on capital, liquidity, and asset-quality indicators (FSF, 2008). However, the global financial crisis of 2007–2009, the pandemic, wars, and geopolitical tensions, as well as mounting climate and cyber threats, demonstrated the need for a holistic approach that also covers organisational, operational, strategic, and reputational factors (KPMG, 2020).

From a financial perspective, equity capital remains the primary determinant (Cavallaro & Villani, 2024). Higher capital levels and the use of regulatory buffers reduce insolvency risk and lower susceptibility to panic propagation. Liquidity mechanisms, contingency funding plans, and diversified funding sources act as complements. The global crisis demonstrated that even valuable assets do not protect against failure in the face of a sudden liquidity shortfall. Digital assets are an increasing challenge: they may undermine monetary sovereignty and generate new liquidity risks. Transmission channels include, inter alia, run risk in stablecoins, margin spirals under high leverage, and liquidity risk in funds with crypto exposure—warranting heightened monitoring and regulatory coordination (Aerts et al., 2025). Another factor is the quality and structure of credit and investment portfolios. Excessive concentration in a single sector—for example, commercial real estate—can drive an increase in non-performing loans (NPLs). Also important is the ability to generate stable income and cash surpluses, supported by diversified revenues, cost optimisation, and technological investment (Gyau et al., 2024; Stoyanov et al., 2025).

Financial institutions' resilience is also shaped by external, systemic factors often beyond the control of individual entities but material to system-wide risk. Particularly notable (Martens, 2023) are as follows:

- Non-bank financial institutions (NBFIs)—they play a growing role in financing the economy and absorbing public debt, yet structural weaknesses (high leverage, liquidity mismatches, USD exposures) heighten sensitivity to global shocks and contagion risk. While the sector has shown resilience to market volatility in recent years, significant exposure to USD-denominated assets means shocks in the US market or foreign exchange (FX) swings can trigger global contagion. NBFIs can thus be both stabilising and destabilising, underscoring the need for stronger macroprudential oversight and coordinated regulation (Martens, 2023).
- Commercial and residential real-estate markets (CRE and RRE)—these are key links in the financial system, as they largely determine banks' credit-portfolio quality and collateral valuations. CRE faces persistently lower demand for office space (remote work), energy-efficiency retrofit costs, and rising vacancies; RRE remains overvalued in many countries. Both segments are sensitive to long-term rates and the cycle; price corrections are quickly transmitted to banks via lower collateral values and higher NPLs (EBC, 2025).

- Client-related factors—their impact on institutions is largely indirect. Panic, bank runs, mass redemptions, or policy cancellations can stem from both real shocks and loss of trust. Rising digital and demographic expectations reshape client relationships and increase operational complexity. Key responses include transparent communication, trust-building, and secure, flexible service models. Population ageing in the EU additionally burdens pension systems and affects labour, capital, and housing markets, requiring efforts to boost productivity, labour-force participation, and the development of market-based retirement savings (FSB, 2024; Gardó et al., 2025).
- Geopolitical uncertainty—the war in Ukraine, other conflicts and tensions (e.g., escalation in Gaza, US–China frictions), and geo-economic fragmentation increasingly shape institutions' risk profiles. Conflicts and sanctions affect balance sheets through trade, FX, and investment channels, while rising defence spending and fiscal pressures constrain states' stabilisation capacity (Kulińska-Sadłocha, 2024). The likelihood of large-scale tail events is rising. Trade-policy tensions and uncertainty worsen banks' funding, asset quality, profitability, and credit growth (Avril et al., 2025; EBC, 2025).

External factors significantly shape the environment in which financial institutions build their resilience. The materialisation of these risks can weaken individual entities or even destabilise the entire financial system; therefore, monitoring such phenomena and incorporating them into resilience analysis is a key element of macroprudential policy (EBC, 2024). Resilience requires accounting for all financial and non-financial factors (internal and external) to ensure the capacity to absorb shocks, adapt, and transform (Cipollone, 2025). All these conditions—from financial to systemic—form the operating framework of financial institutions. Their complexity and interlinkages make regulation and supervision crucial in setting standards, structuring institutional responses, and supporting resilience across the system.

3.4 The role of regulation and supervision in shaping financial resilience

The history of economic and financial crises—from the Great Depression of the 1930s, through the debt crises of the 1980s, to the 2007–2009 global financial crisis—shows that insufficient regulatory frameworks encourage excessive risk-taking, speculation, and contagion effects, which in extreme cases threaten the stability and resilience of entire economies (Martens, 2023). In the past, regulation focused mainly on the microprudential approach aimed at the stability of individual entities. Today, many measures to ensure stability and financial resilience are also undertaken within macroprudential policy, which covers the entire financial system, including interactions and interlinkages among institutions and between the financial system and the real economy (Zioło et al., 2021).

Resilience-shaping regulations have a systemic character and largely concentrate on ten areas important to the resilience of institutions and financial systems, such as financial and operational resilience, consumer protection, systemic risk, retail and wholesale markets, cross-border activity, sustainable development, governance, and the safe use of technology (Figure 3.2).

The multi-level regulatory architecture developed in recent years means that financial resilience is no longer limited to classic capital and liquidity buffers but also encompasses adaptation to climate, social, and technological risks and the implementation of responsible and sustainable business models aligned with the Sustainable Development Goals (SDGs) and the Paris Agreement. The holistic approach combines micro- and macroprudential perspectives, covers financial and non-financial factors, and operates at multiple levels: global, EU, national, and institutional (Table 3.2).

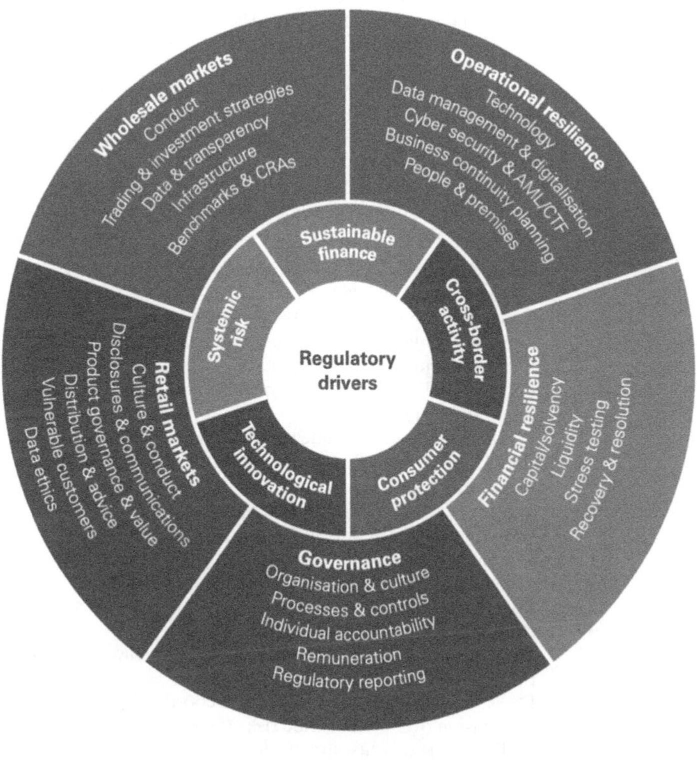

Figure 3.2 A holistic approach to financial resilience regulation.

Source: KPMG (2020).

Table 3.2 Examples of initiatives and regulations strengthening the resilience of financial institutions (global–regional–national–institutional levels)

Level	*Examples and significance*
Global level	Minimum capital and liquidity standards, effective resolution, market transparency, cross-border supervision, and integration of ESG and climate risks. – BCBS—Basel III: higher and better-quality capital requirements, liquidity ratios (LCR, NSFR), leverage ratio; strengthens banks' resilience and reduces systemic risk. – FSB—Key Attributes for Effective Resolution Regimes: frameworks for effective management of failing institutions, ensuring continuity of critical functions without burdening taxpayers. – IOSCO Principles: global standards for capital-market regulation, strengthening transparency, and investor protection. – IAIS—Insurance Core Principles (ICP), ComFrame: supervision of cross-border insurance groups (IAIGs), additional requirements for G-SIIs. – NGFS: integration of climate and ESG risks into central bank and supervisory practice. – FSB—TCFD: recommendations on climate-risk reporting. – UNEP FI—PRB, PSI, PRI: global responsibility principles aligning strategies and business models with the SDGs and the Paris Agreement.
Regional level European Union	Adapting global standards to the EU context, regulatory harmonisation, digital-operational resilience, and integration of ESG and transition finance. – European Green Deal (EGD): strategy to make the EU climate-neutral by 2050. – Strategy for Financing the Transition to a Sustainable Economy: links sector resilience with transition finance, inclusion, and global ambition. – CRR/CRD IV–VI: EU implementation of Basel III (capital, liquidity, leverage). – MAR: market-abuse framework. – BRRD, SRM: orderly bank resolution; bail-in tools, Single Resolution Fund. – Solvency II: risk-based insurance reform (SCR, MCR, ORSA, transparency and reporting). – MiFID II/MiFIR: capital-market transparency, investor protection, regulation of algo-trading and dark pools. – EMIR: central clearing and OTC derivatives reporting, counterparty-risk reduction. – DORA: harmonised digital-operational resilience standards for the financial sector. – ESAs—Guide on DORA Oversight: coordination of supervision over system-wide risks (cyber, outsourcing). – ECB—Guide on outsourcing cloud services. – CSRD, SFDR, EU Taxonomy: ESG and sustainable-finance disclosure obligations. – AIFMD: regulation of alternative funds (hedge funds, private equity).

(*Continued*)

Table 3.2 (Continued)

Level	*Examples and significance*
National level Poland	Adapting EU rules to local conditions, enhancing sector transparency and stability. – Act on Financial Market Supervision: legal basis for the Polish Financial Supervision Authority (KNF). – Act on Macroprudential Supervision of the Financial System and Crisis Management: establishes the macroprudential authority and scope. – KNF Recommendations: for example, on mortgage exposures, retail risk, bancassurance, internal control, and payment security. – Capital and liquidity requirements: aligned with CRR/CRD. – Stress tests: for banks and insurers, including climate and operational risks. – KNF guidelines: ICT risk management, cybersecurity, insurance reserves, and flood risk. – Corporate governance rules: strengthening accountability and transparency in supervised institutions.
Individual Institution level (banks, insurers, investment firms, funds)	Implementing operational tools that ensure financial and operational resilience. – Internal stress tests: recession, liquidity shocks, interest-rate changes. – Implementing operational tools that ensure financial and operational resilience. – Internal stress tests: recession, liquidity shocks, interest-rate changes. – Contingency funding plans: liquidity in crises. – Recovery & Resolution Plans (RRPs): recovery and orderly resolution planning. – Cybersecurity systems (SOC, CERT, CSIRT): defence against attacks and failures. – ESG and climate policies: aligning portfolios and activities with ESG and climate risks.

Source: own elaboration based on Kulińska-Sadłocha (2022), IAIS (2025), information from UNEP FI and individual initiatives' websites.

In the past decade, international organisations, states, central banks, and regulators have intensified efforts to build financial-system resilience and to strengthen coordination and standardisation of processes globally and regionally, including the provision of financing for these efforts (Chortareas, 2023). At the global level, capital and liquidity standards (BCBS, FSB, IOSCO, IAIS), resolution frameworks, and guidelines integrating climate and ESG risks (NGFS) have been established. Also formulated at this level are guidelines and good practices on, inter alia, sustainable business models developed by UNEP FI—Principles for Responsible Banking (PRB), Principles for Sustainable Insurance (PSI), and Principles for Responsible Investment (PRI).

At the regional level—within the European Union—global standards are adapted to the single market and linked to the European Green Deal and the 2030 Agenda. The EU Strategy for Financing the Transition to a Sustainable Economy specifies how the financial sector can strengthen its own resilience while accelerating the Green Deal. The strategy structures actions around transition finance, inclusion, resilience, the sector's contribution to sustainable development, and global ambition. The main tools are credible disclosures, better data and climate scenarios, and anti-greenwashing measures (Krosinsky & Kulińska-Sadłocha, 2025). It compels the development of sustainable business models within financial institutions and the strengthening of system-wide resilience. Key regulations include CRR/CRD, Solvency II, BRRD, MiFID II/MiFIR, EMIR, DORA, and the sustainable-finance package (CSRD, SFDR, EU Taxonomy). Supervisory authorities (ECB/SSM, EBA, EIOPA, and ESMA) play a special role in enabling consistent implementation, limiting regulatory arbitrage, and strengthening early identification of risks across the Union. In June 2025, a political agreement was reached on reforming EU rules on crisis management and deposit insurance (CMDI). The new framework tailors crisis-management tools to the needs and challenges of the banking system—particularly small and medium-sized banks. The reform is expected to make the sector more crisis-resilient, which is essential to Europe's resilience and competitiveness (SRB, 2025).

At the national level in Poland, the most important act is the Act on Financial Market Supervision. Microprudential supervision follows an integrated model (a single authority—KNF—for the entire financial market). The Act on Macroprudential Supervision established the Financial Stability Committee as the macroprudential authority, coordinating the actions of the financial safety-net institutions. The National Bank of Poland (NBP) plays an important role in strengthening system resilience (NBP, 2025). Ultimately, however, it is the institutions themselves—banks, insurers, funds—that are responsible for implementing operational mechanisms such as risk and liquidity management systems, stress testing, recovery and resolution planning, and cybersecurity solutions (Benoit Dupont, 2019; ESMA, 2025).

Despite significant progress, financial-stability reports point to areas requiring further action. Consequently, regulation should continue to (IIF, GFMA, 2021; IMF, 2025; NBP, 2025):

- Strengthen capital buffers and crisis preparedness;
- Cover non-bank institutions, which in many countries have become a comparable source of systemic risk;
- Improve data transparency and disclosure standards;
- Enhance international coordination and develop financial safety nets;
- Limit regulatory arbitrage and accelerate cross-border cooperation.

Recent reports pay particular attention to the NBFI sector—burdened by high leverage and liquidity mismatches—and to the development of crypto-assets, stablecoins, and tokenisation, which increasingly permeate traditional finance (FSB, 2024). In ESG, credible reporting standards are essential to mitigate greenwashing risk. The development of RegTech and SupTech supports the transformation of supervision towards near-real-time monitoring and early threat detection, significantly increasing system resilience. Regulation and supervision thus remain the key mechanisms for strengthening the resilience of individual institutions and limiting risk transmission at the system level (Chortareas, 2023).

3.5 Instruments and tools supporting the resilience of financial institutions

Building resilience requires a set of analytical, managerial, and regulatory instruments that support early identification of threats, assessment of their impacts, and the preparation and execution of response plans in crises (United UNDRR, 2024). This toolkit spans micro- and macroprudential instruments, risk management, and enabling technologies (Table 3.3).

Stress testing plays a key role in assessing the resilience of institutions and of the financial system, serving both micro- and macroprudential objectives (Hirtle et al., 2016). It covers the impact of macroeconomic, market, climate, and operational shocks on banks, insurers, and funds (DeMenno, 2022). Results reveal weaknesses in balance sheets and business models and support decisions on capital, liquidity, and risk strategy (Emambakhsh et al., 2023; Hirtle et al., 2016). In the EU, several types of stress tests are conducted: annual EU-wide tests coordinated by the EBA, thematic stress tests and forward-looking vulnerability analyses, stress tests within comprehensive assessments, and macroprudential stress tests. Those run by the ECB and EBA inform buffer calibration and supervisory decisions (EBA, 2025).

Recovery and contingency plans prepare institutions for risk materialisation, limiting costs to the public sector. They set out sources and sequencing of liquidity mobilisation and include scenarios for reorganisation or orderly resolution; the associated tools increase investor responsibility and limit crisis costs shifted to the public sector. Macroprudential instruments stabilise the system by counteracting imbalances and contagion—acting as a "brake" in booms and a "safety cushion" in downturns (Pyka et al., 2019). Technology tools (RegTech, SupTech, AI, DLT) increasingly automate compliance, support real-time supervision, and strengthen cybersecurity (Aria et al., 2024; Gyau et al., 2024). The financial system is now highly dependent on technology, and even small disturbances can have catastrophic effects on its functioning (Cipollone, 2025). ESG and climate instruments integrate environmental and social risks into risk management, support long-term resilience and sustainable development, and build trust through transparent disclosures.

Table 3.3 Instruments and tools supporting financial resilience (synthetic view)

Group	*Instruments and tools*
Regulatory and macroprudential Objective: enhance loss absorption, limit procyclicality, and contagion	– Capital buffers (conservation, countercyclical, G/D-SIB) – Liquidity ratios LCR/NSFR – LTV/DTI/DSTI limits, sectoral risk weights – For funds and NBFIs (e.g., swing pricing, leverage limits) – BRRD/SRM (recovery plans, bail-in/bail-out, resolution) – Liquidity operations and LOLR – System-wide stress tests – ESG disclosures (CSRD/SFDR/TCFD, EU Taxonomy), verification of transition plans.
Risk management and early-warning systems (ERM + EWS) Objective: coherent decision architecture and effective crisis response	– Three Lines of Defence (business, risk/compliance, audit) – RAF linked to ICAAP/ILAAP – Multi-dimensional stress tests (market, credit, climate) – Early-warning systems (KRIs, ML analytics) – Dashboards and metrics (CET1/TCR, LCR/NSFR, NPL, MREL/TLAC, RTO/RPO, MTTR, WACI) – EWS using financial, client, operational, and cyber data – Contingency Funding Plans; Recovery Plans.
Operational resilience Objective: protect against failures and cyberattacks; ensure continuity	– Business continuity and disaster recovery (BCP/DRP, RTO/RPO) – Location and vendor redundancy, crisis exercises – Third-party risk management (due diligence, SLAs, dependency mapping) – Cybersecurity (penetration tests, red/purple teaming, SOAR/SIEM, MFA, cryptography) – Reliability indicators (MTBF, MTTR, forecast annual unavailability) – Operational monitoring (availability of critical services, "degraded operations" procedures).
Enabling technologies Objective: automate compliance, detect risk, innovate in supervision and settlement	– RegTech (XBRL/API reporting, KYC/AML, policy repositories), SupTech (big-data analytics, model validation, real-time transaction monitoring) – AI/ML (run risk prediction, fraud detection, ESG/climate scoring, portfolio simulation) – DLT/Blockchain (settlement, tokenisation, cycle shortening) – Data architecture (data lineage, data quality, model risk control).
Climate and ESG Objective: integrate sustainability factors and coordinate globally	– Integration of physical and transition risks into ERM – Portfolio vulnerability maps (NGFS) – Sector policies, taxonomy, labels—curbing greenwashing – Transition plans (decarbonisation pathways with KPIs, credibility tests) – Supervisory/policy incentives (e.g., green-asset capital preferences) – Fiscal buffers and FX reserves – Cross-border coordination (supervisory colleges, NGFS, FSB/IMF fora).

Source: own elaboration based on ESMA (2025), EBC (2024), Cavallaro & Villani (2024), ESMA (2022), KPMG (2020), and Bieri (2014).

Measuring financial resilience requires diverse indicators that can be classified as quantitative (e.g., CET1, TCR, LCR, NPL), qualitative (e.g., governance effectiveness, crisis readiness, data quality, third-party risk-management quality), and hybrid measures combining both approaches for a fuller assessment (BIS, 2016; ESMA, 2025). Integrated scoring methodologies that combine financial, operational, and ESG indicators are increasingly used. They support strategic decision-making and enable assessment not only of short-term resilience but also of adaptive and transformational capacity. They can take the form of resilience indices, industry rankings, or internal supervisory scorecards (Daadmehr, 2024; NEF, 2015).

Financial resilience is a system effect: regulation and supervision provide the framework and buffers; central banks provide liquidity and coordination; ERM integrates risks and enforces decision discipline; operations ensure continuity of services; and technology and ESG provide data, detection, and incentives for long-term transformation. Institutions that combine these tools are not only more shock-resistant but also adapt faster and gain competitive advantage.

3.6 Conclusion

Financial resilience is a key attribute of institutions and of the financial system amid rising uncertainty. While stability means maintaining core functions during shocks, resilience additionally entails the ability to adapt and to transform over the long term (Bieri, 2014). Its contemporary understanding is holistic—combining financial and non-financial pillars, integrating regulatory and supervisory mechanisms, and relying on international cooperation. In this sense, resilience enables the financing of the climate and energy transition, innovation, and financial inclusion, strengthening public trust and institutional coherence.

At the institutional level, strong financial foundations (capital, liquidity, portfolio diversification, income stability) must be complemented by non-financial elements—sound management, risk culture, operational resilience, and ESG integration. Equally important are external factors—macroeconomic, geopolitical, sectoral, social, and climate—which, although beyond the direct control of individual entities, materially shape risk profiles and should be systematically integrated into capital and operational planning and into stress testing.

Resilience is built across layers: from global standards (e.g., Basel III, FSB), through EU frameworks (CRR/CRD, BRRD, Solvency II, EMIR, DORA, CSRD/SFDR/Taxonomy), to national regulations and institutional practice. Their common objective is to strengthen absorptive and adaptive capacity through capital and liquidity buffers, resolution mechanisms, macroprudential tools, and the integration of climate and digital risks. The development of RegTech/SupTech and predictive analytics is shifting supervision from periodic reporting towards continuous monitoring.

International reports highlight priority actions for the coming years (EBC, 2025; IMF, 2025; NBP, 2025):

- Integrating traditional financial metrics with non-financial measures and operational resilience;
- Calibrating capital and liquidity buffers also beyond the banking sector;
- Developing RegTech/SupTech and predictive analytics for early risk detection;
- Treating geopolitics, climate, cybersecurity, and demographics as integral components of risk management;
- Strengthening cross-border cooperation to limit regulatory arbitrage.

Building resilience is a systemic process requiring the cooperation of financial institutions, central banks, regulators, governments, and stakeholders. Only in such a configuration can the financial system maintain stability, build resilience, and develop a lasting capacity for learning, adaptation, and support of sustainable socio-economic development. The development of both financial markets and financial institutions constitutes two fundamental pillars of system resilience, providing the capacity to absorb shocks and long-term support for the real economy (Tang et al., 2022).

References

Aerts, S., Born, A., Gati, Z., Kochanska, U., Lambert, C., Reinhold, E., & van der Kraaij, A. (2025). Just another crypto boom? Mind the blind spots. *Financial Stability Review*, May. https://www.ecb.europa.eu/press/financial-stability-publications/fsr/special/html/ecb.fsrart202505_01~62255f2625.en.html, (accessed: 17.08.2025).

Aria, J., Jose, D., Diego C., William, B., & Enoch, O. (2024). *The Role of AI in Shaping Financial Institutions' Response to Emerging Risks*, December. https://www.researchgate.net/publication/387079664 (accessed: 12.08.2025).

Atkins, L., Banerjee, S., Boer, M., Craig, L., Greis, J., Hao, G., & Idler, M. (2024). *The Cyber Clock Is Ticking: Derisking Emerging Technologies in Financial Services*. McKinsey, March 11. https://www.mckinsey.com/capabilities/risk-and-resilience/our-insights/the-cyber-clock-is-ticking-derisking-emerging-technologies-in-financial-services (accessed: 15.09.2025).

Avril, P., Bochmann, P., Fahr, S., Horan, A., Pancaro, C., & Pizzeghello, R. (2025). Risks to Euro area financial stability from trade tensions. *Financial Stability Review*, May. https://www.ecb.europa.eu/press/financial-stability-publications/fsr/special/html/ecb.fsrart202505_02~4603d3e42a.en.html (accessed: 15.09.2025).

Benoit Dupont, B. (2019). The cyber-resilience of financial institutions: significance and applicability. *Journal of Cybersecurity*, Vol. *55*, October. https://www.researchgate.net/publication/336425785_The_cyber-resilience_of_financial_institutions_significance_and_applicability (accessed: 17.08.2025).

Bieri, S. (2014). *Conceptualizing Financial Resilience*. Conference Paper. VT Ridenour Faculty Fellowship Conference Arlington, VA. October https://www.researchgate.net/publication/269986256 (accessed: 26.09.2025).

BIS. (2016). *Economic Resilience: A Financial Perspective*, 16 December. https://www.bis.org/publ/othp27.pdf, (accessed: 17.08.2025).

Cavallaro, E., & Villani, I. (2024). Financial resilience, growth and risk sharing in the EU. *International Economics*, Vol. *180*. https://www.sciencedirect.com/science/article/pii/S2110701724000738 (accessed: 17.08.2025).

Chortareas, G. (2023). Global financial architecture: Structures and transformations. *Business and Economics Journal*, Vol. 14. https://www.hilarispublisher.com/open-access/global-financial-architecture-structures-and-transformations.pdf (accessed: 17.08.2025).

Cipollone, P. (2025). What resilience takes: strengthening the financial system in an era of heightened risk. Keynote speech by Piero Cipollone. *Member of the executive board of the ECB*. At the Resilience Conference hosted by De Nederlandsche Bank. Amsterdam, 17 September. https://www.ecb.europa.eu/press/key/date/2025/html/ecb.sp250917_2~279de8d776.en.html (accessed: 15.09.2025).

Colloff, M.J., Martín-López, B., Lavorel, S., Locatelli, B., Gorddard, R., Longaretti, P.Y., Walters, G., Van Kerkhoff, L., Wyborn, C., Coreau, A., & Wise, R.M. (2017). An integrative research framework for enabling transformative adaptation. *Environmental Science & Policy*, Vol. *68*. https://www.sciencedirect.com/science/article/pii/S1462901116301289 (accessed: 27.07.2025).

Daadmehr, E. (2024). Workplace sustainability or financial resilience? Composite-financial resilience index. *Risk Management*, Vol. 26. https://link.springer.com/article/10.1057/s41283-023-00139-9 (accessed: 20.09.2025).

DeMenno, M. (2022). Environmental sustainability and financial stability: can macroprudential stress testing measure and mitigate climate-related systemic financial risk? *Journal of Banking Regulation*. https://link.springer.com/article/10.1057/s41261-022-00207-2 (accessed: 18.06.2025).

Dobrzańska, A., Kosycarz, E., & Pietrzak, B. (2017). *Stabilność systemu finansowego w gospodarce – rozważania teoretyczne i praktyczne aspekty*. In *Mechanizmy stabilności systemu finansowego*, ed. A. Alińska and K. Wasiak. Wydawnictwo Beck.

Duchek, S. (2020). Organizational resilience: A capability-based conceptualization. *Business Research*, Vol. *13*. https://link.springer.com/article/10.1007/s40685-019-0085-7 (accessed: 25.09.2025).

EBA. (2025). *EU-Wide Stress Tests – Result*, 1 August. Raport. https://www.eba.europa.eu/sites/default/files/2025-08/0178b9c5-2f0d-42ee-8226-6fa0a87c0d6c/2025%20EU-wide%20stress%20test%20-%20Results.pdf accessed: 15.09.2025).

EBC. (2024). *Raport roczny EBC z działalności nadzorczej 2024*. https://www.bankingsupervision.europa.eu/press/other-publications/annual-report/html/ssm.ar2024~700cba1314.pl.html (accessed: 12.05.2025).

EBC. (2025). *Financial Stability Review*, May. https://www.ecb.europa.eu/press/financial-stability-publications/fsr/html/ecb.fsr202505~0cde5244f6.en.html (accessed: 15.08.2025).

EC. (2019). Communication from the Commission to the European Parliament, the Council, the European Economic and Social Committee and the Committee of the Regions. *The European Green Deal*. https://eur-lex.europa.eu/legal-content/EN/TXT/?qid=1576150542719&uri=COM%3A2019%3A640%3AFIN (accessed: 30.06.2025).

EC. (2021). Communication from the commission to the European Parliament, the Council, the European Economic and social committee and the committee of the regions. *Strategy for Financing the Transition to a Sustainable Economy*. https://eur-lex.europa.eu/legal-content/EN/TXT/?uri=CELEX:52021DC0390 (accessed: 30.06.2025).

Emambakhsh, T., Fuchs, M., Kördel, S., Kouratzoglou, Ch., Lelli, Ch., Pizzeghello, R., Salleo, C., & Spaggiari, M. (2023). *The Road to Paris: Stress Testing the Transition towards a Net-Zero Economy*. Occasional Paper Series. No 328. ECB. https://www.ecb.europa.eu/pub/pdf/scpops/ecb.op328~2c44ee718e.en.pdf?7793485730460e4e0b4e170237eb7429 (accessed: 18.06.2025).

ESMA. (2022). A Framework to assess operational resilience. *TRV Risk Analysis* 19 December. https://www.esma.europa.eu/sites/default/files/library/esma50-165-2155_-_trv_-_operational_resilience_for_financial_institutions.pdf, (accessed: 22.12.2025).

ESMA. (2025). Operational and cyber risks in EU financial markets: measurement and stress simulation. *TVR Risk Analysis*, 17 July. https://www.esma.europa.eu/sites/default/files/2025-07/ESMA50-1949966494-3823_TRV_risk_article_-_Operational_and_cyber_risk_measurement_and_modelling.pdf (accessed: 15.08.2025).

FSB. (2024). *Depositor Behaviour and Interest Rate and Liquidity Risks in the Financial System: Lessons from the March 2023 Banking Turmoil*, 23 October. https://www.fsb.org/uploads/P231024.pdf (accessed: 12.08.2025).

FSF. (2008). *Report of the Financial Stability Forum on Enhancing Market and Institutional Resilience*, 7 April. https://www.bafin.de/SharedDocs/Downloads/EN/Rundschreiben/dl_fsf_enhancing_resilience_en.html, (accessed: 11.07.2025).

Gardó, S., Klaus, B., Kurig, D., & Storz, M. (2025). Navigating financial stability in an ageing world. *Financial Stability Review*, May. https://www.ecb.europa.eu/press/financial-stability-publications/fsr/special/html/ecb.fsrart202505_03~9db108da0e.en.html (accessed: 12.08.2025).

Gyau, E. B., Appiah, M., Gyamfi, B. A., Achie, T., & Naeem M. A. (2024). Transforming banking: Examining the role of AI technology innovation in boosting banks financial performance. *International Review of Financial Analysis*, Vol. *96*. https://www.sciencedirect.com/science/article/pii/S105752192400632X (accessed: 21.06.2025).

Hirtle, B., Kovner, A., Vickery, J., & Bhanot, M. (2016). Assessing financial stability: The Capital and Loss Assessment under Stress Scenarios (CLASS) model. *Journal of Banking and Finance*, Vol. *69*. https://www.sciencedirect.com/science/article/abs/pii/S0378426615002940 (accessed: 12.08.2025).

IAIS. (2024). *Insurance Core Principles and Common Framework for the Supervision of Internationally Active*. December. https://www.iais.org/uploads/2025/06/IAIS-ICPs-and-ComFrame-December-2024.pdf, (accessed:12.08.2025).

IIF. GFMA. (2021). *Priorities for Strengthening Global Operational Resilience Maturity in Financial Services*, 28 January. https://www.iif.com/portals/0/Files/content/Regulatory/01_28_2021_op_resilience.pdf (accessed: 17.08.2025).

IMF. (2025). *Financial Stability Report, Enhancing Resilience Amid Uncertainty*. Washington, DC. April. https://www.imf.org/-/media/files/publications/gfsr/2025/april/english/text.pdf

Jeans, H., Castillo, G.E., & Thomas, S. (2017). *The Future Is a Choice Absorb, Adapt, Transform Resilience Capacities*. Oxfam International, January https://oxfamilibrary.openrepository.com/bitstream/handle/10546/620178/gd-resilience-capacities-absorb-adapt-transform-250117-en.pdf;jsessionid=E2E93751B85FA5656D142F824477753F?sequence=4 (accessed: 17.08.2025).

KPMG. (2019). *Operational Resilience in Financial Services*. Seizing Business Opportunities, June. https://assets.kpmg.com/content/dam/kpmg/xx/pdf/2019/06/operational-resilience-in-financial-services.pdf (accessed: 17.08.2025).

KPMG. (2020). *Financial Resilience in Banking: A Balancing Act*, December. https://assets.kpmg.com/content/dam/kpmg/xx/pdf/2020/12/financial-resilience-in-banking.pdf (accessed: 11.06.2025).

Krosinsky, C., & Kulińska-Sadłocha, E. (2025). Climate finance. In *Finance, ESG and Sustainability: Contemporary Issues in Finance*, ed. M. Ziolo and M. Zaleska. Routledge.

Kulińska-Sadłocha, E. (2022). Environmental regulations as a framework for environmental risk management in banks. In *Environmental Risk Modelling in Banking*, ed. M. Ziolo. Routledge International Studies in Money and Banking. London: Routledge.

Kulińska-Sadłocha, E. (2024). Wpływ wojny w Ukrainie na funkcjonowanie banków w Polsce. In *Społeczna Gospodarka Rynkowa w dobie transformacji energetycznej w Unii Europejskiej i Ukrainie*, ed. E. Mączyńska, P. Pysz and M. Urbaniec. Warszawa: Wydawnictwo Polskiego Towarzystwa Ekonomicznego.

Martens, J. (2023). *Reforms to the Global Financial Architecture Proposals, Conflicts and Prospects on the Way to the Summit of the Future 2024 and the Financing for Development Conference 2025*. GPF. December. https://www.globalpolicy.org/sites/default/files/download/Briefing_Reforms%20to%20the%20global%20financial%20architecture.pdf (accessed: 12.08.2025).

Mullan, M., & Ranger, N. (2022). *Climate-Resilient Finance and Investment: Framing Paper*. OECD Environment Working Papers. No. 196. OECD Publishing. Paris. https://doi.org/10.1787/223ad3b9-en (accessed: 18.06.2025).

NBP. (2025). *Raport o stabilności systemu finansowego. czerwiec* https://nbp.pl/wp-content/uploads/2025/06/Raport-o-stabilnosci-systemu-finansowego.-Czerwiec-2025-r.pdf, (accessed: 15.09.2025).

NEF. (2015). Financial system resilience index. Building a strong financial system. *Report*. https://new-economicsf.files.svdcdn.com/production/files/70470851bfaddff2a2_xem6ix4qg.pdf, (accessed: 15.09.2025).

Olsson, L., Jerneck, A., Thoren, H., Persson, J., & O'Byrne, D. (2016). Why resilience is unappealing to social science: Theoretical and empirical investigations of the scientific use of resilience. In *The Routledge Handbook of International Resilience*, ed. D. Chandler, and J. Coaffee. Article 5.

Pyka, I., Zygierewicz, M., Bolibok, P., & Nocoń, A. (2019). *Polityka makroostrożnościowa w regulowaniu stabilności sektora bankowego: innowacyjność, implementacja, bariery*. Katowice: Prace Naukowe Uniwersytet Ekonomiczny w Katowicach.

Soliwoda, M. (2020). *Odporność z perspektywy ekonomii i finansów. Wybrane problemy*. Wydawnictwo: Instytut Ekonomiki Rolnictwa i Gospodarki Żywnościowej. Warszawa.

SRB. (2025). *SRB Statement: Crisis Management and Deposit Insurance Political Agreement*. https://www.srb.europa.eu/en/content/srb-statement-crisis-management-and-deposit-insurance-political-agreement, (accessed: 26.09.2025).

Stoyanov, A., Imregun, D., Noteboom, P., & Brown, J. (2025). *Banking on the Next Generation. A Playbook for US Midcap Banks*, September 16. MCkinsey & Campany Financial Services. https://www.mckinsey.com/industries/financial-services/our-insights/banking-on-the-next-generation-a-playbook-for-us-midcap-banks (accessed: 20.09.2025).

Tang, C., Xiaoxing Liu, X., & Zhou, D. (2022). Financial market resilience and financial development. A global perspective. *Journal of International Financial Markets, Institutions and Money*, Vol. *80*. September. https://www.sciencedirect.com/science/article/abs/pii/S1042443122001226, (accessed: 15.09.2025).

Tanner, T., Bahadur, A., & Moench, M. (2017). *Challenges for Resilience Policy and Practice*. London: Overseas Development Institute. https://www.researchgate.net/publication/319645442_Challenges_for_resilience_policy_and_practice, (accessed: 17.08.2025).

United UNDRR. Standard Chartered Bank. KPMG International. (2024). *Guide for Adaptation and Resilience Finance*, 11 April. https://www.undrr.org/media/95342/download?startDownload=20250928 (accessed: 12.08.2025).

Zioło, M., Spoz, A., & Kulińska-Sadłocha, E. (2021). *Zrównoważone rynki finansowe, Perspektywa krajowa i międzynarodowa*. Warszawa: *PWE*.

4 Sustainable Development Goals (SDGs) and financial resilience in the EU-27

Romania's regions of development – A case study and policy insights

Diana-Mihaela Țîrcă, Isabel Novo-Corti, Cornelia Dumitru, and Xose Picatoste

4.1 Introduction

The current period is dominated by complex uncertainties, volatility, and the (re)shaping of most institutions governing the economic, social, and political spheres. The macroeconomic challenges at the global level have increased, in particular over the past five years, as we regard the year 2019 as the end of an economic, social, and political cycle. The next period, which we consider transformative for all markets, was triggered by the outbreak and consequences of the pandemic, whose effects persist to this day and may have contributed to the rise in geopolitical instability, as open conflicts continue in Europe (the Russian–Ukrainian war) and the Middle East.

In this context, Europe as a whole is faced with multiple challenges, while the European Union is faced with the task of managing the repercussions of being in the immediate proximity, which poses new questions about resilience and sustainability in general, thereby affecting goals and targets that sometimes are overlapping or adjacent to the Sustainable Development Goals of the United Nations.

The adaptive economic resilience of the EU is expressed in how the economic policies are pursued to ensure not only stability but also to take into account security concerns, especially in areas that converge with the Sustainable Development Goals (SDGs) adopted in the 2030 Agenda for Sustainable Development.

The proposed universal framework addressed three relevant dimensions: economic, social, and environmental challenges that have to be mitigated in order to ensure increased stability and welfare at global and European levels. From the EU-27 perspective, the 17 SDGs require for

DOI: 10.4324/9781003648840-4

their achievement an improved regulatory framework corresponding to the EU standards, ensuring a favorable and stable business environment, transparency, and good governance, as there are multifaceted challenges such as energy transition, digital transition, and green transition, which all contribute to ensuring resilience and sustainability. Moreover, achieving these goals requires significant financial resources and targeted interventions aimed at strengthening the capacity of banks, investment funds, and insurance companies to act not only as financial intermediaries but also as key drivers of change, by encouraging and supporting technological and social innovation, as well as policies and strategies that enhance global resilience and sustainability.

Hence, financial institutions play a pivotal role, as the allocation of resources, risk management, and market incentives pertain to their core objectives and activities. However, in the case of the European Union and of its member-states, an increased concern is noticeable regarding the outcomes of the past five years, resulting in the emergence of increased direct key systemic risks such as cyber threats, disruptions in the payment systems, the emergence of non-bank financial institutions (NBFI), macroeconomic shocks that result from increased protectionism trends, and geopolitical fragmentation. To these are added indirect systemic risks related to green transition, energy transition, social inequality, and the overall shift to a new and even more complex system based on the evolving digital economy and society.

As a result, over the past four years and looking ahead to the foreseeable future, the EU-27 has faced increasing pressure to strengthen financial resilience and self-reliance in order to mitigate adverse impacts on both businesses and households. In this context, several initiatives have been undertaken, including the Savings and Investments Union (SIU), which aims to create financial opportunities for EU citizens while simultaneously channeling savings toward productive investments. This horizontal instrument seeks to enhance Europe's capacity to mitigate current and future uncertainties and volatility, while also taking into account geopolitical dynamics that will require substantial investment. In fact, the Draghi report estimates an additional 750–800 billion per year by 2030. This report on EU competitiveness also addresses the fact that in the immediate future industry and companies of the single market will require additional investments, in particular the small- and medium-sized enterprises and innovative firms that are faced with complex issues and choices, and not always able to rely on bank financing alone. Hence, the horizontal mechanism created by SIU could be a way of facilitating a direct and effective connection between savings and investment needs. The form is that of a Savings and Investment Account (SIA) addressed to citizens who can invest based on amounts such as small as 10 euros for long-term goals, for growth in conditions of balance and transparency. SIA is accessed by means of the regulated financial services providers, including traditional and online banks, allowing the control of citizens over the financial products and economic sector, and on the grounds of the investor protection rules. From among the member-states where SIA has already been implemented, we mention France with the Plan d'épargne en actions that will be used as an SIA scheme and Sweden, with the Investeringssparkonto, while Poland is in the process of preparing the implementation.

Based on this legal instrument, banks, insurance companies, and investment firms—indeed, all financial entities—can withstand, respond to, and recover from Information and Communication Technology (ICT) disruptions, thereby addressing operational resilience in the financial sector.

It is obvious that the mentioned aspects indicate that also the economic institutions, as defined by North (North, 1991), representing the main EU markets will need to be readjusted and reshaped, as they are a relevant contributing component to long-run economic growth (Acemoglu et al., 2005), but also to societal development, and implicitly to resilience and sustainability.

In fact, the quality of institutions is relevant for how the Environmental, Social, and Governance (ESG) will operate in the future as EU-27 framework of reference for investments that prioritize environmental issues, social issues based on the foundations resulting from absorbing Corporate Social Responsibility (CSR) by all corporations, and enterprises operating within the EU-27, including financial institutions. In fact, this is the root of impact investing. Actually, by providing the first basic mechanisms and gradual implementation of the ESG, the EU-27 might be regarded as initializing a new institutional innovation that is considered a useful tool in implementing, in a harmonized manner, the required policies, measures, and actions that assist in achieving EU-level goals and the UN SDGs.

The following sections addressing the financial resilience of financial institutions are structured in line with the main research objective. First, the theoretical framework is presented, providing the conceptual justification for the proposed approach and reviewing relevant contributions from the specialized literature. Examines the state of the art of the EU-27 financial system, with a particular focus on the resilience of financial institutions and their role in supporting the achievement of the Sustainable Development Goals (SDGs). Presents a case study on Romania, analyzing regional development disparities at the NUTS 2 level in order to highlight persistent challenges and risks that affect financial resilience and, implicitly, progress toward the SDGs. The fifth section discusses policy recommendations and outlines directions for future research, while the final section concludes by summarizing the main insights for strengthening not only the resilience of EU financial institutions but also that of European societies in the context of ongoing multifaceted transitions aligned with the SDGs.

4.2 Theoretical framework

The complex context of global economies and societies is generated by the global need to ensure resilience and sustainable development and to mitigate emerging economic, social, and environmental challenges. However, the beginning of the second decade of the 2000s brought with it the outbreak of a pandemic, and the first open conflict on the European continent and in the immediate proximity of the EU-27 borders after the Second World War. Both events have contributed to signaling the fact that 2019 was the last year of an economic, social, and political cycles as conditions have changed on all markets – goods, services, capital, and even labor markets – with significant implications for financing needs at national/regional and global levels, for investments and investment flows, in a context dominated by swift technological changes triggering not only economic effects but also social impacts.

Even if resilience and sustainability are already well-established concepts, the current period justifies a brief review of their definitions, as a backbone for a more integrated systems thinking required by the current economic and social context, in which SDGs and financial institutions have the role of ensuring stability and opening new ways for the prosperity of global societies.

Resilience – the first concept of interest was the result of the research by C.S. Holling in the field of ecology, as he defined it as the measure in which systems persist and are able to absorb change and disturbance, thereby maintaining the same relationship between populations or state variables (1973), simplified to the ability of a system to absorb any disturbances and still maintain function and structure (Walker et al., 2006), to which might be added that resilience is "the capacity to change and still maintain the same identity" (Folke et al., 2010). Another way of looking at resilience, this time from an economic and social perspective, is to consider it as the capacity of the socio-economic and financial systems faced with macro-level structural shocks to mitigate these shocks and to continue delivering according to expectations regarding societal well-being in ways that continue to be sustainable (Manca et al., 2017). The key attributes of resilience are therefore absorption, adaptation/adjustment, and transformation/shift, to which, in the case of financial resilience, we might add the ability of the financial systems (at national and EU levels) to enhance constant growth and international risk sharing (Cavallaro et al., 2024).

Resilience is directly linked to the other two relevant concepts: *systems thinking* and *sustainable development*.

Systems thinking might be interpreted in two ways: either by approaching in a holistic manner the components contained inside it, based on the relationships between them, and their effects on each other, or by reflecting on how separate systems, or parts of their components, interact with other systems and their components. In both cases, this delivers insights, and possibly surprising inferences based on the interdependencies, feedback loops, and patterns of generating interactions and relationships. Thus, systems thinking is a way of approaching complex issues when decision-making processes need to be improved, based on the analyses highlighting opportunities, challenges, and risks that need to be dealt with, allowing also for establishing priorities, for instance, based on multi-criteria decision-making (MCDM) methods.

Sustainable development was defined as the ability to meet present needs of societies without compromising future needs by searching and identifying ways that ensure balance in the case of competing economic, social, and ecological goals. With respect to financial systems, it may be regarded as the capacity and capability of the financial institutions to act responsibly and adopt measures and safeguards dedicated to preventing irresponsible banking or use of damaging financial instruments. In this context, an ongoing debate is related to the emerging Social and Sustainable Finance (SSF), a rather new field of research for interested academics and experts, and many aspects require further investigation.

This approach also emphasizes how much broader in scope and collective action are the SDGs against the Millennium Development Goals (MDGs) as they include a larger number of priorities requiring the collective action of stakeholders from the public and private sectors based on the identified 169 targets and 230 indicators that show high level of interconnectedness in all areas that require attention in undertaking actions as to meet health, social, and economic benefits (Tosun et al., 2017). At the same time, the SDGs developed in 2015 shift more responsibility toward the private sector, implying the need for the financial sector to direct resources toward capacity building, technology, making good use of available data, and relying on the support of institutions (Morton et al., 2017). Hence, this results in a direct link of interest between sustainable development and sustainable business issues affecting aspects related to production and productivity, to the businesses' impact on climate and their responsibility in preventing climate change, and to ensuring that by their actions they contribute to creating sustainable cities (Rizzello & Kabli, 2020).

In this context, considering the high financing needs required by the SDGs, another potential gap is identified that might be closed by laying more emphasis on reconsidering the way in which public–private partnerships and cooperation operate, especially within the EU-27, as the contribution of the private funding sources continues to be scarce and less aligned with the SDGs (Dalby et al., 2019), despite registering some progress in the past decade (Lehner, 2016), and indicating the validity of introducing social and sustainable perspectives and reasons in the process of investing.

This theoretical framework consisting of how resilience in the digital economy and society should be configured in relation to the SDGs based on a systems thinking approach that allows for making good use of tools that highlight, by mixed economic and social methods, how the SDGs fit in the overall EU-agenda on one hand and on the other hand how this type of approach brings about the opportunity of better integrating industry, business, and governmental interests and objectives with the interests of the general public and of the societies concerned with the welfare and well-being not only for the present but also for the future.

Based on tools such as SIU, its product SIA, and DORA, together with the provisions contained in the ESG, a clear link emerges between the SDG financing needs and the requirement for the resilience of financial institutions, as shown in Figure 4.1.

While financial institutions allocate resources to SDG-related projects through instruments such as green bonds, microfinance, and impact investing, this action generates reactions for multiple stakeholders and thus effects and impacts are distributed either inside a single system or to more systems that deliver responses from increased diversification of products to generating innovation and contributing to increased institutional quality by building improved reputation, for instance through compliance, and thus having a share in increasing the reputation, stability, and trust in the EU and national economy. In brief, these actions that are measurable in terms of capital, generation of new resources, and market and profit stability contribute to stronger financial resilience, which in turn is measurable by indicators such as higher capital adequacy, improved liquidity, better asset quality, and more stable profitability. In this way, the pursuit of SDG financing is not merely a CSR activity but a

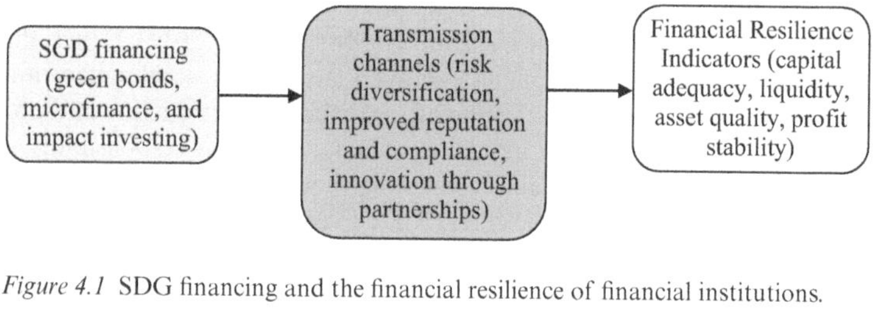

Figure 4.1 SDG financing and the financial resilience of financial institutions.

strategic mechanism for enhancing the long-term robustness of financial institutions.

4.3 EU-27 financial resilience of financial institutions and SDGs – case study Romania's regions of development

The EU-27 has been forced by the evolutions of the past five years to evolve and even consider adding a new dimension to the resilience and sustainability framework. Hence, in addition to the economic, social, environmental, and institutional dimensions, the geopolitical dimension is increasingly taken into account, especially in key areas such as European financial stability, and energy transition, both relevant for the EU – innovation and competitiveness capabilities. The geopolitical dimension becomes relevant for its impact on businesses and households, as it increases and adds to the geoeconomic volatility, which already has contributed to a diminished economic sentiment. This means that the financial market sentiment is affected and displays major shifts, just like the economic one.

Within the EU, most geopolitical threats and acts have increased consistently, especially post-2010 (Figure 4.2), and have been reflected in the cyberattacks that target state institutions and critical infrastructures, thus exposing member-states to systemic disruptions. The risks have increased

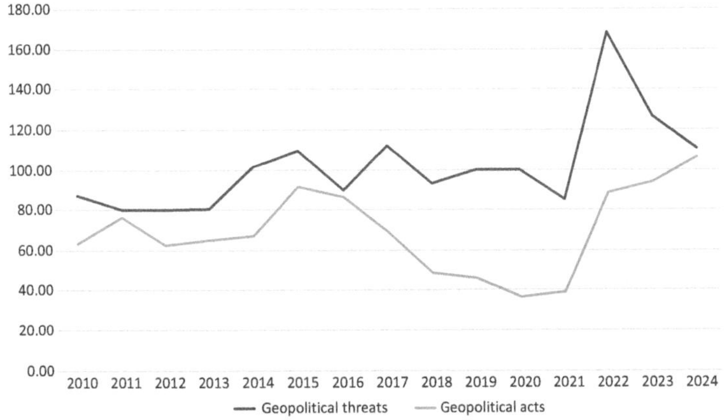

Figure 4.2 Geopolitical threats and geopolitical acts over the period 2010–2025.

Source: author's own processing after ECB calculations based on Caldara and Iacovello, "Measuring Geopolitical Risks" *American Economic Review*, Vol. 112, No. 4, April 2022, pp. 1194–1225. EuRepoC database.

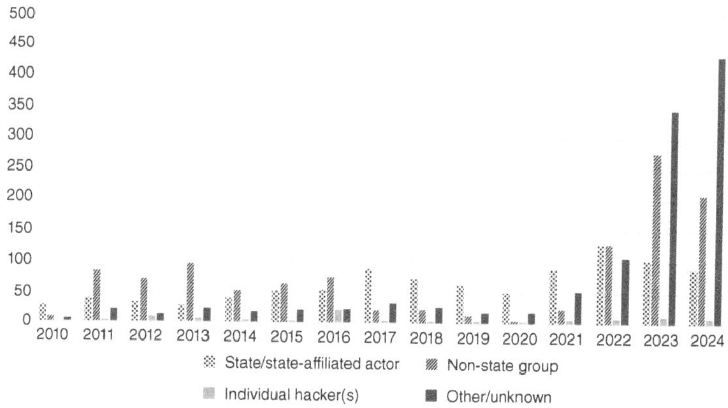

Figure 4.3 Cyberattacks by threat actor type.

Source: author's own processing after ECB calculations based on Caldara and Iacovello, "Measuring Geopolitical Risks" *American Economic Review*, Vol. 112, No. 4, April 2022, pp. 1194–1225. EuRepoC database.

constantly since the beginning of the 2000s, and based on these evolutions, it becomes even clearer that 2019 was the end of a cycle, even in this respect (Figure 4.3).

It is noticeable that the period of the financial-economic crisis and the first post-crisis years showed relative stability regarding geopolitical threats and geopolitical acts, with a slight peak due to the events of 2014 (the Crimean Russian invasion), the migration wave of 2015, and the perceived risk triggered by the 2016 Brexit referendum.

Another fact that is relevant in analyzing cyber threats is obvious, namely that most of them are performed by non-state groups, and other/unknown actors. The increase in their attempts post-2022, which due to interconnectedness and increasingly higher digitalization of the economies, pose a substantial threat to financial stability due to the fact that such actions could lead to operational disruptions, propagating effects to businesses, and households alike, and thus undermining trust in the EU's financial institutions, and their capacity to answer to financing needs of the SDGs. Hence, the geopolitical dimension is not only a threat to financial stability but also to the stakeholders in the financial sector involved in various actions that support the SDGs, and the new ESG framework set as a mechanism at the EU-27 level, which shares a set of commonalities with the SDGs (Table 4.1).

A clarification is required at this point: the realization of SDGs is dependent on the collective action of public and private sectors, their

Table 4.1 TFEU, SDGs, and key systemic areas

Dimension	*TFEU Provisions*	*SDGs*	*Objectives*
Sustainability	Sustainable Development: Part I, Title I, Art. 3, letters d, e, i, k; Art. 4, letters e, i, k; Title II, Part I, Title I, Art. 3, letters d; Art. 4, letters e, i, k; Art. 11 (amended, former Art. 6 of TEC*).	SDG 8 – decent work and economic development, 9 – industry, innovation, and infrastructure, 12 – responsible consumption and production, 13 – climate action	Triple bottom objective: people, planet, profit All these imply strengthening resilience and ensuring financing resources, by investments or other innovative solutions agreed on between stakeholders of the public and private sectors.
Social Inclusion	Title X, Art. 156 (art. 140, TEC), Art. 160 (art. 144, TEC), Title XII, Art. 165 (149 from TEC), Item 2, Art. 166, Item. 2, social equity, education, employment, and social protection, etc.	SDG 1 – no poverty, 2 – no hunger, 3 – good health and well-being, 4 – quality education, 5 – gender equality, 10 – reduce inequalities	Representative for the main areas of intervention that outline a necessary shift toward increased involvement of the private sector, from large corporations to SMEs, in identifying financial and other resources for ensuring the progress of the European society.
Environmental Protection	Title XX, Art. 191 (previously Art. 174 TEC), item 1, up to and including Art. 193 (previously 176 TEC)	SDG 6 – clean water and sanitation, 12 – responsible consumption and production, 13 – climate action, 15 – life on land	Environmental protection, quality of life in urban areas, reducing the carbon footprint, and circular economy
Governance	Title II, Art. 15, Part 6, Title 1, Section 7, art. 285 and cont., Ch. 2, Section 1, and 2, communication, ethical governance, transparency, and accountability of EU bodies	SDG 16 – peace, justice, and strong institutions, 17 – partnerships for the goals	Leadership and ethical management of businesses, economic and financial accountability, prevention of corruption, and enhancing the role and flexibility of partnerships for realizing the goals.

Source: authors' own processing.

financing capacity, and the trust between the two main sectors in cooperating transparently, a fact that sends a positive message to the general public that they cooperate. The evolving area of ESG (Environment, Social, Governance), in fact a superior and improved variant of CSR, especially in the second decade of the 2000s, only stresses how the EU aims to take a qualitative leap in fulfilling the demands of the SDGs by incorporating them in a judicious manner into the preexisting framework of the Treaty on the Functioning of the European Union (TFEU), and improving the frameworks – based on ESG – for pursuing them according to the SDG 2030 Agenda (2015).

Table 4.1 highlights clearly that there are considerable links between economic, social, and environmental objectives and targets, and that the adoption of the ESG as a working mechanism is currently a necessary requirement, to which several member-states of the EU still have to adjust. Additionally, given the high volatility and uncertainty generated by ongoing geopolitical disturbances—such as trade barriers, tariffs, and open conflicts—at both the EU-27 and member-state levels, it is advisable, over the medium to long term, to include the geopolitical dimension when assessing progress or challenges. Geopolitical factors affect the functioning of economic and social institutions and can have consequences for economic and social outcomes across all member states.

For example, we relate our analysis to SDG Goal 8, namely decent work and economic growth, as essential for ensuring both financial stability and increased participation of public and private stakeholders, and of the societies of the member-states. The option was focused on target 8.1, respectively, to sustain per capita economic growth in accordance with the national circumstances, which also highlights impacts that trigger effects for financial stability, as well.

It is noticeable from the presented Sankey diagram (Figure 4.4) that there are multiple synergies and multiple trade-offs that impact the other SDGs.

This is relevant because the implementation of the SDGs at the national level is conditioned by considerable variations, influenced by the pace of economic growth, the institutional quality, and the priorities specific to the respective member-states. For instance, Northern European countries, such as Finland, Denmark, and Sweden, consistently rank highest in SDG achievement, with Finland as the leader for several consecutive years. On the other hand, southern and Central and Eastern Europe (CEE) member-states have been lagging behind (Bulgaria, Italy, Romania) in fields such as energy transition and security, and regarding the decrease of their carbon footprint, overall. At the same time, by its nature, Goal 8 and all its sub-summed targets are essential and key systemic indicators for the well-functioning of other components, from financing and investment capacity of the public and private sectors, to their openness and willingness to cooperate, and ability to form coalitions

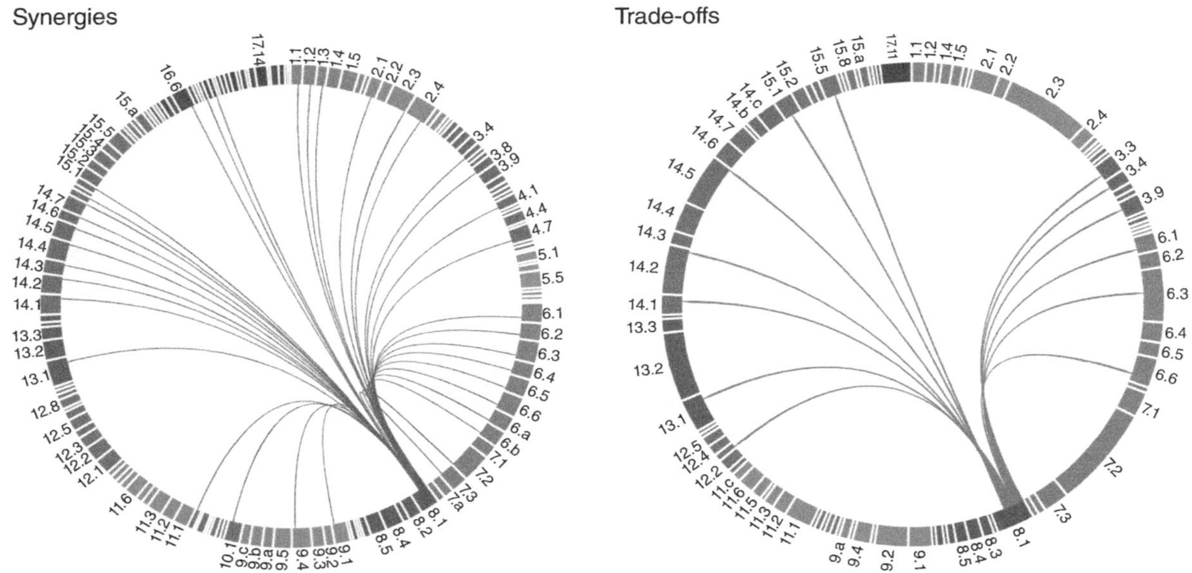

Figure 4.4 Decent work and economic growth according to national circumstances.

Source: authors' own processing based on Interlinkages – targets|KnowSDGs (europa.eu).

and partnerships for ensuring resilience and sustainability at national, and as consequence, at EU-27 level.

One other relevant aspect, to which more attention should be paid, is the fact that national performance and competitiveness, along with the capacity of delivering on the necessary economic, social, and environmental capabilities depend on the potential of the regions of development of the respective countries, and the level of disparities registered between the respective regions of development from within each and any of the member-states. We argue that achieving the SDGs in line with the EU's resilience and sustainability agenda depends on whether the development regions (NUTS 2) of member states possess the capacities and capabilities needed to meet both national and EU-27 objectives concerning overall and financial stability, as well as EU goals relevant to the SDGs.

Overall, the EU-27 shows good scores regarding the realization of the SDGs, with the latest data available for the year 2023 indicating either maintaining their position based on the calculated score or improvements. However, when looking at the "no one left behind" scores, which are relevant in particular for goal 8 in correlation with Goals 1, 2, 3, 4, and 10, it is concerning that some countries, in particular southern and eastern-European member-states indicate that they keep lagging, and there is a considerable risk in this gap increase (Figures 4.5 and 4.6).

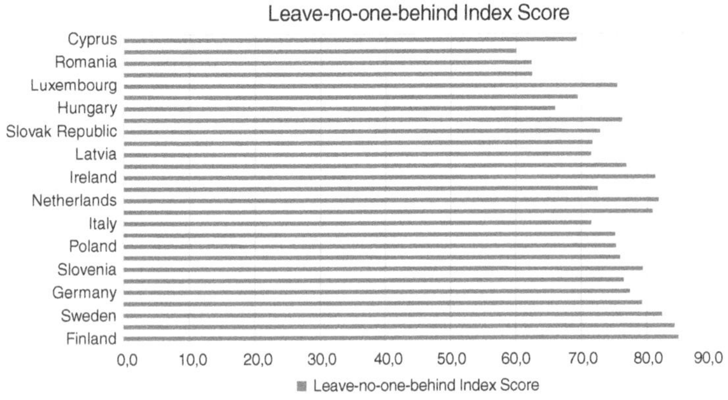

Figure 4.5 SDG index score.

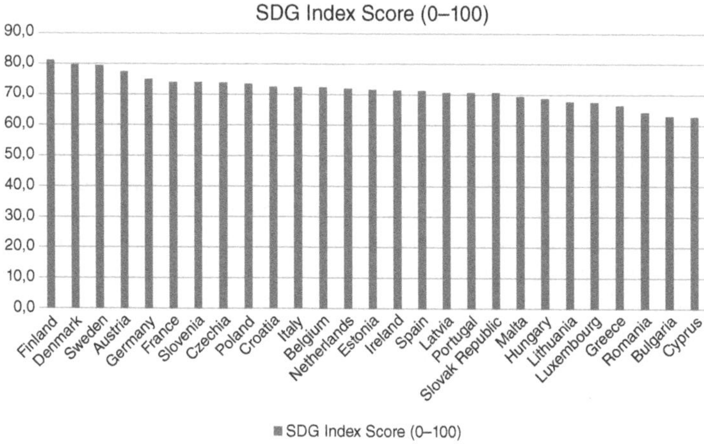

Figure 4.6 Leave no one behind index score.

Source: authors' own processings after, esdr_2025_online_database, for the Europe Sustainable Development Report, 2025.

Hence, in the next chapter, we suggest an analysis based on the regions of development (NUTS2) for Romania, a country that shows many specificities in the context of EU accession and integration.

4.4 Case study: Romania's regions of development

Romania has had a difficult path in integrating fully into the EU, as challenges were encountered since accession (2007), only a brief period before the first signs of the financial–economic crisis were felt in Europe, and the EU as well. After the economic and financial crisis, Romania resumed growth, and its convergence and cohesion processes ensured that catching-up was progressing. However, difficulties were and are still present, most being derived from fragilities in institutional quality, and several delays in complying with commitments, especially regarding budgetary deficits, while lagging in the absorption of EU funds dedicated to convergence and cohesion.

Nevertheless, the country is part of the efforts to realize the SDGs, based on the National Strategy for Sustainable Development, which is the main framework for aligning national targets with the SDGs, and on National Action Plans, aimed at better integrating national and SDG objectives. The latter are the main tools for operationalizing the strategies into measures, by establishing also terms, finalization timelines, and the responsible institutions/entities.

While governance and coordination are entrusted to central and regional authorities, who also initiate collaboration with representatives of the civil society, the academy, and the private sector, the most relevant are the policy instruments by which SDG targets are integrated into sectoral strategies. In this context, the main financing sources are provided by the EU Cohesion policy funds and, post-2020, the funds that were provided for the National Recovery and Resilience Plan (NRRP) on grounds of the mechanism instituted by the Recovery and Resilience Mechanism (RRM). These funds are the main source for large public investments, such as green infrastructure, digital services, and social inclusion. The domestic contribution from public budgets is dedicated mostly to social protection, education, and health. Additional support is granted by means of international finance (foreign direct investments), the World Bank, and European Bank for Reconstruction and Development (EBRD), the latter supporting projects for territorial sustainable development.

However, it is noticeable that sustainable development and resilience vary at the level of the Romanian regions of development (North-East, North-West, South-West, South-East, South-Muntenia, Bucharest-Ilfov, West, and Centre), with increasing discrepancies among these regions and Bucharest-Ilfov taking a leading position, but without visible spillover effects to its immediate vicinities.

Therefore, considering that national outcomes are finally the result of the aggregated outcomes obtained at the level of the regions of development, we propose mapping the correlation between SDG, financial stability/fintech, and EU-27 targets based on a number of six selected indicators, respectively: GDP per capita, in public–private partnerships (PPS), as percentage of EU as of the year 2020, unemployment rate for the age group 20–64, at-risk-of-poverty rate, household internet access, tertiary education rate for the age group 20–64, and life expectancy at birth, over the period 2021–2023, based on data availability. Figure 4.7 represents the evolution of the six indicators over this time frame.

It is obvious that Bucharest-Ilfov leads, followed by the West and South-West sub-national levels. Most striking is the fact that the GDP per capita (28,300 eur) was almost more than double the Romanian average (12,600 eur), and more than three times that of the region with the weakest performances (North-East, about 8,300 eur). In fact, this development region of Romania is the most challenged one, regarding main infrastructures, and has the highest need for additional investments.

From the perspective of infrastructures, investments, and demographic potential, the most attractive regions, leaving aside Bucharest-Ilfov, are

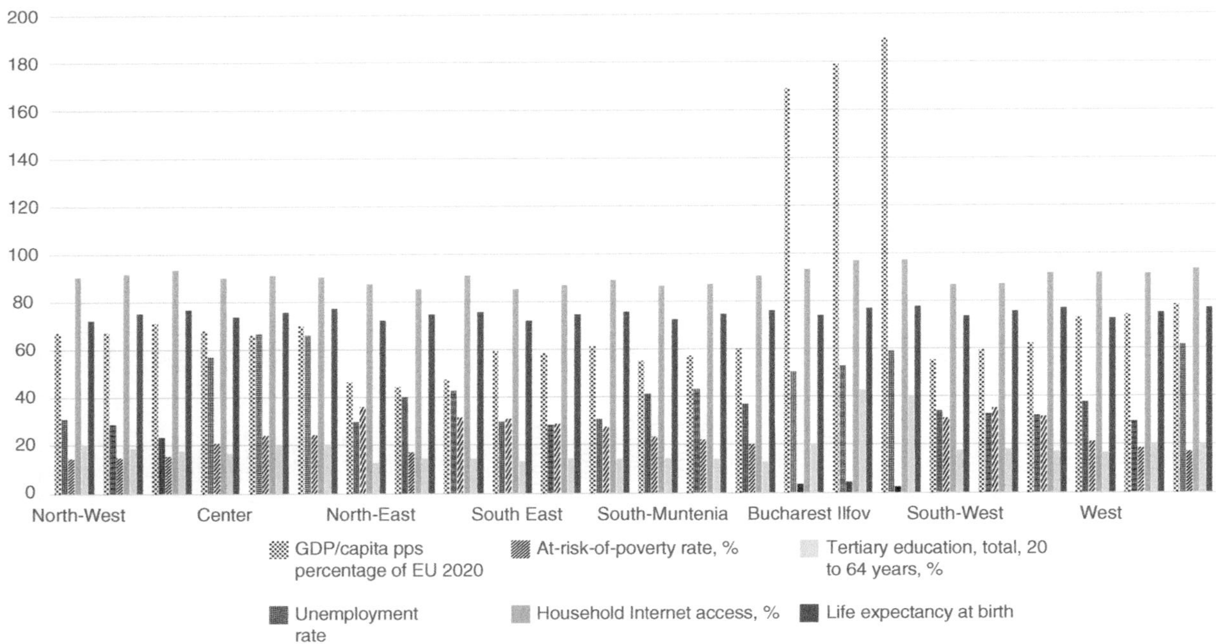

Figure 4.7 Evolution of key indicators for the Romanian regions of development over the period 2021–2023.

Source: authors' own processing, after Eurostat data.

the West and North-West regions. These regions are also the best performers regarding innovation, infrastructure, and human capital, existing and potential.

These considerable differences have strong implications for SDG delivery and the financial stability of the country, in particular regarding the attractiveness of the regions for direct and foreign direct investments. In fact, these visible disparities should represent the basis for initiating a national platform for investigating the potential of cooperation between public authorities at all levels (central, regional, and local) and the private sector for improving the conditions in the regions of development, so as to reduce the gap between them and the Bucharest-Ilfov region.

Table 4.2 Analysis of intervention needs and SDGs on regions of development

Region	*Key strengths*	*Key weaknesses/ challenges*	*Priority SDGs and interventions required*
Bucharest-Ilfov	Strong economy, high GDP per capita, better infrastructure, more innovation capacity, higher quality services.	Potential inequalities even within the region; pressures of urbanization (housing, pollution, traffic); maybe saturation of some services; risk of neglecting outskirts.	SDGs related to sustainable cities (11), infrastructure and innovation (9), climate action (13), quality education and decent work (4, 8) – invest in urban sustainability, green transport, manage growth smartly.
West, North-West, Centre	Better infrastructure, more diversified economies, somewhat higher levels of human capital, proximity to EU markets.	Still lagging behind Bucharest-Ilfov, parts of rural areas disadvantaged, sometimes weaker institutional capacity, less developed coastal or mountainous areas.	SDGs linked to economic growth, infrastructure, education, reduced inequalities (10), sustainable consumption and production, environmental protection, improve connectivity, rural service provision, innovation ecosystems.

(*Continued*)

Table 4.2 (Continued)

Region	*Key strengths*	*Key weaknesses/ challenges*	*Priority SDGs and interventions required*
South-West South-Muntenia, South-East, North-East	Rich natural landscapes; in some cases, agricultural potential; cultural heritage; opportunities for tourism, natural resource-based economies.	Very high poverty and social exclusion, weak infrastructure (transport, digital), low innovation levels, aging and migration, low service access in rural areas.	SDGs like No Poverty (1), Zero Hunger (2), Reduced Inequalities (10), Clean Water and Sanitation (6), Affordable and Clean Energy (7), Climate Action, Quality Education, Health; levers include targeted EU funds, improving access to public services, capacity building, strengthening rural economic diversification.

Source: authors' own processing.

Table 4.3 Descriptive statistics

	N	*Minimum*	*Maximum*	*Mean*	*Std. deviation*	*Variance*
GDP/capita pps, % EU 2020	24	44	190	76.46	40.775	1662.607
Unemployment rate, 20–64yrs., %	24	22.9	66.5	40.775	13.214888	174.633
At-risk-of-poverty rate, %	24	2.1	35.5	21.420833	9.470227	89.685
Household Internet access, %	24	85.09	96.93	90.150833	3.2947533	10.855
Tertiary education, total, 20–64 yrs., %	24	12.3	42.2	19.041667	8.7413021	76.41
Life expectancy at birth	24	72	77.6	74.829167	1.701273	2.894
Valid N (listwise)	24					

Source: authors' processing after Eurostat data.

Table 4.4 Principal component analysis

Total variance explained

Component	*Initial eigenvalues*			*Extraction sums of squared loadings*			*Rotation sums of squared loadings*		
	Total	*% of variance*	*Cumulative %*	*Total*	*% of variance*	*Cumulative %*	*Total*	*% of variance*	*Cumulative %*
1	3.945	65.752	65.752	3.945	65.752	65.752	3.200	53.330	53.330
2	0.911	15.182	80.934	0.911	15.182	80.934	1.304	21.725	75.055
3	0.713	11.878	92.812	0.713	11.878	92.812	1.065	17.757	92.812
4	0.262	4.371	97.183						
5	0.148	2.467	99.651						
6	0.021	0.349	100.000						

Source: authors' own processing after Eurostat data in SPSS v. 26.

The discussion should specifically address the strengths and weaknesses, and the alignment with the priority SDGs, implicitly with the EU-27 targets (Tables 4.2–4.4).

It is obvious that all regions of development require tailored solutions for closing existing gaps and reducing their lag at the national level, and subsequently in comparison with the other EU regions of development. Therefore, in order to identify key patterns, trends, and types of interventions required, we performed a two-step Principal Component Analysis (PCA) analysis. The first PCA analysis of the indicators mentioned above was conducted to provide a clear picture of broad socio-economic development and, specifically, the well-being dimension, while the PCA restricted to 2023 aimed to highlight the potential of fintech and the requirements for achieving higher financial stability at the regional level.

The first step was cleaning and standardizing the data for the PCA analysis, which delivered the following results based on the z-scores that were kept as variables:

In this way, three PCs were extracted, respectively, PC 1 reflecting the overall socio-economic development, which explains 65.75% of the variance, as it loads positively on GDP per capita, internet access in households, and tertiary education. Hence, it is significant for the targets related to less poverty. PC 2 is a reflection on the employment/labor dimension, where the unemployment rate is responsible for only 15.1% of the outcomes, thus contributing to separating the regions by their employment/unemployment performance relative to other characteristics. Finally, PC 3 captures some of the undetected, residual contrasts (e.g., at-risk-of-poverty rate against other indicators, which might explain smaller, yet regional-specific structural differences), including demographic consequences and sustainability.

The analysis shows that GDP per capita, tertiary education, and household internet access contribute to diminishing poverty, while the unemployment rate could be regarded as capturing the trade-offs between labor market stress and social safety actions.

For introducing a synthetic Fintech proxy, we resorted to an alternative solution, due to the lack of enough reliable data about Fintech use in Romania, at the level of the regions of development.

The average national Fintech use was used as a proxy and maintained constant, at 0.27772, based on Eurostat/World Bank and NBR data. The formula used was:

$$\text{Fintech Proxy Region} = \left(\text{Household Internet Access Region} / 100\right) \times \text{National Fintech Use Rate.}$$

5 ESG and financial resilience

Filippo Grasso and Daniele Schilirò

5.1 Introduction

Environmental, Social, and Governance (ESG) criteria are essential for evaluating an organization's performance in terms of sustainability, which is inherently a multidimensional concept.

ESG criteria are the key pillars and a framework for evaluating how an organization (company or institution) performs in these three critical areas. With growing social pressure and heightened environmental concerns about climate change, the world is increasingly focused on sustainable practices, making ESG criteria more important than ever for investors and businesses. Furthermore, ESG elements have become integral to the field of sustainable finance (Chang et al., 2022; Martiny et al., 2024; Schilirò, 2020; Zairis et al., 2024; Ziolo et al., 2021). Consequently, the relationship between ESG and sustainable finance is fundamental, as is the connection between ESG and financial resilience (Ameur & Boussetta, 2023).

Financial resilience refers to an organization's ability to withstand and adapt to economic disruptions or crises, while maintaining operational continuity, liquidity, and investor confidence during challenging periods.

In recent years, an emerging consensus has developed: undertaking an ESG shift is crucial for meeting new compliance regulations and gaining a competitive advantage. ESG criteria have become significant for helping companies mitigate environmental risks and enhance brand premiums. Consequently, they have garnered growing interest from investors and financial institutions (Ni et al., 2024). Given the central role of the financial sector in the overall economy and the fact that banking is the single largest profit-generating sector in the world, the ESG behavior of banks and other financial organizations has come under increased scrutiny. Studies examining the channels through which ESG activity impacts bank value have found a positive relationship between ESG activity and both cash flows and efficiency (e.g., Azmi et al., 2021).

DOI: 10.4324/9781003648840-5

This chapter primarily analyses the relationship between ESG criteria and financial resilience by examining theoretical literature and providing practical insights. It also discusses the broader relationship between ESG and sustainable finance, as ESG has become a key driver of sustainable finance growth.

5.2 Methodology and focus of the chapter

The methodology adopted in this chapter is primarily conceptual in nature. It critically examines ESG criteria and financial resilience, particularly emphasizing their interrelationship. The objective is to synthesize existing concepts, offer multi-level perspectives, and contribute to a broader and more nuanced understanding of the topic. A comprehensive review of the relevant literature elucidates the connections between these constructs and identifies the key challenges associated with their integration. While not intended to be exhaustive, this chapter seeks to advance scholarly discourse by facilitating a deeper exploration of these complex and increasingly significant domains. However, through a detailed examination of the role and significance of individual ESG factors within the strategic frameworks of financial institutions, this chapter seeks to advance a more comprehensive understanding of these constructs, promote their critical appraisal, and evaluate their influence on financial resilience, as well as the attendant complexities and challenges.

5.3 The ESG framework of reference

ESG stands for Environmental, Social, and Governance and refers to the three key criteria for measuring an investment's sustainability and ethical impact. As MSCI (2024) pointed out, ESG investing began in the 1960s as an evolution of socially responsible investing. During this time, investors began excluding activities harmful to society and countries that did not align with certain principles. For instance, they excluded stocks or entire industries from their portfolios based on business activities such as tobacco production or involvement in the South African apartheid regime.

Peterdy (2024) emphasizes that ESG is a framework designed to help stakeholders understand how an organization manages risks and opportunities related to environmental, social, and governance factors. Thus, ESG reflects a governance responsibility rather than merely serving as a communications tool. It is crucial for sustainability, as it promotes responsible business practices that help preserve resources for future generations. ESG takes a holistic approach, recognizing that sustainability encompasses more than just environmental concerns. Additionally, the term is widely used in capital markets, where investors rely on it to evaluate corporate behavior and anticipate future financial performance.

The environmental component of ESG assesses how an organization interacts with the natural environment and surrounding ecosystems. This evaluation includes considerations such as efforts to reduce pollution and emissions and strategies for conserving natural resources. Such assessments enable investors to gauge an organization's environmental sustainability and commitment to reducing its ecological footprint. De Sousa Barbosa et al. (2023) review the existing literature on the impact of ESG integration on corporate sustainability performance. Their findings indicate that incorporating ESG criteria—analyzed from multiple perspectives—contributes positively to achieving corporate sustainability outcomes. Furthermore, Khalil et al. (2024) highlight the impact of environmental performance on corporate sustainability and solvency.

The social element of ESG delves into how an organization engages with various stakeholders, including the communities in which it operates. It considers factors such as promoting diversity and inclusion within its workforce or upholding human rights standards throughout its operations. This aspect of ESG evaluation aims to assess the organization's impact on society beyond its financial performance, emphasizing its responsibilities toward stakeholders and broader societal well-being. For instance, Gehrig et al. (2024) find significant empirical evidence that social responsibility contributes to increased bank resilience. They predict banks with higher ESG ratings perform better and pose fewer prudential concerns for supervisory authorities during crises.

Governance focuses on how an organization is managed and overseen. This includes, among other things, examining the leadership structure, protecting shareholder rights, and ensuring transparency and accountability in decision-making processes. It also involves addressing issues such as corruption and managing legal matters to uphold ethical standards and ensure compliance with laws and regulations. Governance and macroeconomic conditions are crucial for financial stability and resilience. This is particularly evident for banks, which require stable financial systems to support sustainable growth (Ullah et al., 2024).

It is important to assess an organization's ESG performance. This involves examining how it impacts the environment, handles waste, manages its workforce, and promotes diversity within its leadership.

As reported in DataSnipper (2024), understanding a company's ESG performance helps investors assess its sustainability and risk management. Transparent ESG reporting enables investors to make informed decisions and encourages companies to prioritize ESG factors. Transparency is crucial in ESG reporting, as organizations should be open about their ESG practices. This helps investors understand their investments and holds organizations accountable for their actions.

Groups such as research firms and credit agencies rate organizations on ESG performance. Unfortunately, comparing these ratings can be difficult because no standardized methodology exists.

As highlighted by Li et al. (2023), the role of ESG criteria in shaping investment choices has gained prominence in recent years, as investors recognize their significance in assessing a company's long-term viability and risk management. This increased focus on ESG performance has led to a change in basic assumptions in investment behavior, with more investors considering non-financial metrics alongside traditional financial indicators. Similarly, Kräussl et al. (2023) note that, over the past 15 years, investor interest in ESG investments has grown steadily. This development can generate significant implications, given the role of investor preferences in determining risk premia and their term structures.

The motivations driving investors to incorporate ESG considerations into their portfolio allocation decisions are diverse. For example, in their survey of institutional investors, Krueger et al. (2020) highlight that reputation, moral or ethical considerations, legal/fiduciary duties, and financial motives all play a role in integrating climate risk into portfolio decisions.

Regarding performance, Doherty et al. (2023) find that companies enhancing their ESG performance can achieve higher growth and profitability while delivering superior returns to shareholders. Specifically, their findings reveal that companies that outperform their peers in growth and profitability while also improving sustainability and ESG scores—referred to as "triple outperformers"—achieve annual excess Total Shareholder Returns (TSR) that are two percentage points higher than those of companies excelling only in financial metrics. TSR is a measure of financial performance, representing the total return an investor gains from an investment in equities or shares of stock. It includes price appreciation and any dividends paid during the performance period, which are expressed as a percentage. Therefore, their analysis of TSR, financial performance, and ESG ratings across 2,269 public companies demonstrates that firms with robust growth and profitability, alongside improvements in sustainability and ESG, outperform their peers in both growth and shareholder returns.

Yu et al. (2024) present a study that examines the relationship between ESG performance and investment mix, revealing a significant positive impact of ESG performance on capital investment. The study emphasizes that earning-driven investments, particularly capital projects with a strong ESG focus, can align financial objectives with sustainable practices, enhancing long-term viability and stakeholder trust. However, the findings highlight the complexities of balancing financial goals with environmental responsibilities, underscoring the need for a strategic approach that reconciles these objectives while considering the trade-offs between investment mix and ESG performance.

Not only is the existence of ESG criteria important in companies' investment decisions, but the impact of ESG disclosure is equally significant. As Xue (2025) highlighted, regulators should leverage market forces and disclosure requirements to achieve a Pigouvian tax-like effect—encouraging companies to internalize the externalities associated with climate-related investments.

Kräussl et al. (2023) criticize frameworks for modeling ESG investor preferences that treat ESG investors as a homogeneous group. In their view, socially responsible investors may differ in their preferences across various aspects of sustainability, or they may have heterogeneous priors and distinct beliefs about a firm's sustainability performance. They also argue that research should focus on measuring investors' subjective perceptions of firms' sustainability performance. Another critical issue is whether ESG investors are misinformed and act on inaccurate expectations rather than genuine preferences for sustainability. Additionally, they emphasize that future research should focus on effective methods for detecting greenwashing and designing mechanisms to penalize firms or funds that engage in such practices. Studies in this area would help inform policymakers about the effectiveness of ESG-focused regulations.

More recently, in the context of the COVID-19 pandemic, Al Azizah and Haron (2025) highlight the critical role of ESG performance in fostering organizational resilience and facilitating long-term value creation. Their study indicates that the financial implications of ESG initiatives are highly context-dependent and shaped by broader macroeconomic conditions. These findings underscore the importance of developing adaptive ESG strategies aligned with financial sustainability goals, offering essential implications for corporate executives, investors, and policymakers seeking to navigate the complexities of the post-pandemic economic environment.

5.4 Financial resilience

As mentioned above, this contribution focuses on understanding the connection between ESG and financial resilience.

Van Der Vegt et al. (2015) define financial resilience as the ability of a financial market or system to withstand and quickly recover from external shocks effectively. In other words, it refers to an institution's capacity to endure and adapt to economic disruptions or crises, such as recessions, market volatility, or global events like the COVID-19 pandemic. According to Broto and Lamas (2020), financial resilience encompasses two primary aspects: the ability to absorb and recover from shocks. Financially resilient institutions can maintain liquidity, ensure operational continuity, and uphold investor confidence during challenging times.

Empirical studies by Broadstock et al. (2021), Engelhardt et al. (2021), and Yang et al. (2024) suggest that high ESG values help reduce risk during financial crises. Their findings indicate that financial assets with strong ESG performance are risk mitigation instruments, enhancing financial resilience.

Financial resilience refers to a bank or other financial institution's ability to withstand shocks, maintain stable operations, and sustain long-term profitability. Capital adequacy and risk management have traditionally been the primary focus areas. However, ESG factors are increasingly recognized as key drivers of long-term financial performance and resilience.

Let us examine how individual ESG factors contribute to financial resilience.

Environmental factors encompass climate change, resource depletion, pollution, and regulatory compliance. Climate change presents both physical and transition risks. Physical risks stem from the increasing frequency and severity of extreme weather events, which can damage physical assets, disrupt operations, lead to loan defaults (e.g., mortgages in flood zones), and raise insurance costs. Transition risks arise from policy shifts toward a low-carbon economy—such as carbon taxes and stricter regulations on polluting industries—which can impact investment portfolios and lending strategies. Assets in carbon-intensive sectors (e.g., fossil fuels) may become stranded, leading to financial losses.

When considering financial resilience, institutions that fail to address climate risks may face asset devaluation, operational disruptions, and impaired loan portfolios, ultimately weakening their financial position. Conversely, those integrating climate considerations into lending, investment, and risk models can strengthen resilience and unlock new opportunities in green finance.

Regarding resource depletion and pollution, resource scarcity and stricter environmental regulations can affect the viability of specific sectors (e.g., mining, agriculture) that financial institutions lend to or invest in. Also, financing projects linked to deforestation or severe pollution can damage a financial institution's reputation, leading to customer attrition and potential restrictions on market access. To ensure resilience, lenders and investors must assess the long-term sustainability of business models. Ignoring these issues can expose institutions to declining industries, regulatory penalties, and reputational harm, ultimately undermining financial stability. Finally, regarding regulatory compliance, it is important to emphasize that proactively addressing environmental concerns helps financial institutions avoid legal penalties and regulatory hurdles. Strong environmental compliance reduces financial and operational risks and fosters investor confidence and long-term stability.

The social factor relates to human capital and productivity. The social factor also influences consumer trust and brand loyalty, as ethical labor practices and community engagement enhance a company's reputation and customer retention. Finally, it contributes to risk mitigation, as strong social policies reduce the likelihood of labor strikes, discrimination lawsuits, and reputational damage (Ziolo et al., 2019). From a financial resilience perspective, strong social performance can enhance an institution's reputation, foster customer loyalty, and improve employee productivity and retention. In particular, organizations that invest in their workforce are more likely to be innovative, adaptable, and resilient to market changes. By prioritizing employee well-being, diversity, and inclusion, they tend to experience higher engagement and lower turnover, leading to cost savings and increased productivity. Conversely, a lack of focus on human capital can result in talent shortages and higher staff turnover, negatively impacting operational efficiency and performance.

Furthermore, organizations that adopt robust ESG practices tend to demonstrate stronger financial resilience by proactively addressing risks related to climate change, resource depletion, regulatory compliance, and reputational challenges. Additionally, ESG-focused organizations often earn greater loyalty from customers, employees, and investors, providing a buffer during economic downturns. These organizations also enjoy better access to capital, as investors increasingly favor ESG-aligned businesses, allowing them to secure funding more easily and benefit from lower financing costs. Furthermore, ESG practices enhance operational efficiency through sustainable resource management and effective governance, driving cost savings and streamlining operations (Schilirò, 2019; Schilirò, 2024). Finally, ESG fosters long-term value creation by driving innovation and adaptability in dynamic markets, ultimately promoting sustainable growth (Madgavkar, 2024; Zumente & Bistrova, 2021). As a result, ESG is no longer just a measure of corporate responsibility but a strategic imperative that enhances financial resilience. By embedding ESG principles into their core operations, organizations can better withstand economic downturns, attract investment, and drive long-term success.

The governance factor encompasses various aspects, such as risk management and compliance. Good governance ensures strong internal controls, reducing fraud, corruption, and mismanagement. Compliance with regulations minimizes the risk of fines and legal issues. Conversely, weak risk management and inadequate compliance are detrimental to resilience, as they can lead to financial losses and regulatory penalties, severely impacting an institution's ability to survive crises. Effective governance also enhances investor confidence by promoting transparency in financial reporting and ethical business practices, which attract long-term investors and ensure the proper conduct of financial audits. Additionally, effective governance supports strategic decision-making, leading to stronger corporate strategies and greater resilience against economic downturns. Conversely, increased vulnerability to risks, poor strategic decisions, and reduced accountability can weaken an organization's ability to navigate crises. At the same time, diverse and independent boards offer a broader range of perspectives, enhancing strategic decision-making and improving overall governance.

A study by Hamid et al. (2023) focusing on an emerging market (i.e., Malaysia) identified that financial knowledge and inclusion are significant predictors of financial resilience. Individuals with higher financial literacy and access to various financial products were more likely to be financially resilient. The authors also highlighted that financial resilience varies across socio-demographic groups, suggesting that targeted financial education and inclusion initiatives could enhance resilience among vulnerable populations.

If we were to summarize the overall impact of ESG on financial resilience, we could assert that organizations with strong ESG practices tend to experience lower volatility in financial performance due to proactive risk management, greater access to capital as investors prioritize ESG-compliant firms, and enhanced adaptability in responding to economic, environmental, and regulatory change.

ESG factors should not be treated as separate side issues; they must be integrated into core business strategies, risk assessments, and investment processes. Additionally, ESG considerations are often long-term drivers of value creation and risk reduction. Organizations that adopt a short-term focus risk missing valuable opportunities and becoming more vulnerable to systemic risks. While regulatory compliance is essential, organizations must go beyond mere adherence and proactively integrate ESG principles to drive positive outcomes and gain a competitive advantage.

By actively addressing ESG factors, organizations, particularly financial institutions, can strengthen their financial resilience, attract responsible investors, and contribute to a more sustainable and equitable economy. Neglecting these factors is irresponsible and increasingly detrimental to long-term financial performance and stability.

Furthermore, financial resilience needs to be measured. However, measuring financial resilience is a complex task, which has led researchers to develop multidimensional measurement approaches. In this context, Kamble et al. (2025) propose an ex-ante measure that assesses individuals' capacity to mitigate the impacts of adversities by utilizing appropriate resources. This method emphasizes the importance of proactive financial planning and resource availability in building resilience.

Among its numerous implications, financial resilience is increasingly recognized as a critical factor in shaping social and public health policies. Okumu et al. (2024) indicate that financial inclusion—such as a savings account—and financial literacy are associated with improved financial resilience. These findings suggest that policies promoting financial education and access to financial services can enhance individuals' ability to cope with economic challenges, thereby contributing to broader societal well-being.

5.5 ESG for financial resilience

ESG criteria have increasingly been recognized as critical components of financial resilience, particularly in economic shocks, climate-related risks, and societal disruptions. Specifically, ESG scores are derived from various metrics and indicators associated with environmental, social, and governance factors, quantitatively assessing a company's performance across these dimensions. However, the heterogeneity of ESG methodologies raises questions regarding comparability and reliability, as different frameworks may produce divergent assessments of the same firm (Chen et al., 2023). While ESG practices are often credited with enhancing organizational resilience—by promoting sustainable resource use, ethical labor practices, sound governance structures, and long-term risk mitigation—the extent to which they translate into measurable financial performance remains contested. Although evidence suggests that ESG can positively influence corporate outcomes, concerns persist that ESG ratings may reflect disclosure quality rather than substantive practices, thereby introducing risks of "greenwashing." Consequently, while ESG performance increasingly informs investment decisions, lending criteria, and insurance considerations, its role should be critically examined within the broader financial ecosystem. As Marsh (2024) emphasizes, organizations that adopt a proactive and systematic approach to ESG integration may strengthen their resilience; nevertheless, companies that fail to articulate a coherent and credible ESG strategy risk undermining the viability and legitimacy of their operations in the long term.

Empirical studies suggest that firms with strong ESG performance tend to exhibit a lower cost of capital, reduced downside risk, enhanced value preservation, and greater financial resilience during periods of crisis (e.g., Al Azizah & Haron, 2025; Ameur & Boussetta, 2023; Doherty et al., 2023).

However, Mita et al. (2024) report findings indicating a negative association between ESG performance and financial resilience. In their view, ESG initiatives may be less valuable during a crisis because they consume financial resources, suggesting that organizational survival takes precedence over sustainability. Furthermore, Sergi (2024) emphasizes that corporate carbon emissions are influenced by the presence of reporting on environmental expenditure investments; it follows that the presence of governance and the environmental orientation are relevant factors.

Moreover, the environmental factor for financial institutions—as reflected in the transition to green financing—is crucial for an organization's reputation and is increasingly becoming a global regulatory requirement.

On the social side, criteria examining how an organization treats and values its employees and surrounding communities—such as labor management policies, health, safety, and well-being commitments—are just a few of the many concerns for financial institutions (Ziolo et al., 2019). Additionally, the need to embed diversity and inclusion policies, promote social equality, and ensure customer privacy is crucial. Taking these factors into account is a testament to social resilience.

Regarding governance, ESG criteria are particularly relevant as they provide a framework for assessing an organization's corporate governance practices. These criteria promote accountability, transparency, and sound decision-making. Key focus areas include board structure—especially board diversity—audit quality, transparency, and executive remuneration. Adherence to governance principles is essential for ensuring an organization's financial resilience. Strong corporate governance frameworks, characterized by effective board oversight, ethical leadership, robust risk management, and alignment of executive incentives with long-term performance, enhance a firm's capacity to withstand economic shocks and uncertainties. Firms with high governance standards are better positioned to anticipate and mitigate emerging risks, maintain investor confidence, and respond effectively to regulatory and market changes. Moreover, empirical evidence (e.g., Tricker, 2022; Doherty et al., 2023; Wang et al., 2024) suggests that strong governance reduces the likelihood of corporate misconduct and financial distress, thereby enhancing a firm's overall stability and capacity to retain value during periods of crisis. As such, governance is central to ESG performance and foundational to developing resilient financial systems.

Furthermore, organizations that adopt a proactive and systematic approach to understanding the impact of the three ESG factors and climate change on their most valuable assets will be better positioned to embed greater resilience into their operations. Importantly, climate change should not be viewed merely as a subset of the environmental pillar of ESG but rather as a cross-cutting issue that influences all dimensions of ESG.

Among the key actions to take, organizations should assess the implications of ESG by leveraging industry data, risk indices, physical climate models, and stakeholder perspectives. They should analyze and establish measures to manage the physical, transition, and reputational risks associated with ESG. In addition, organizations should evaluate the need for external reporting, as many financial institutions worldwide are already aligning with established reporting frameworks.

5.6 Reporting and measurement of ESG-related financial resilience

This section examines the reporting and measurement of ESG-related financial resilience—a topic that links sustainability with financial strength and risk management. Organizations increasingly rely on international

ESG reporting frameworks to disclose and assess resilience (Dauerer, 2025). In practice, financial institutions and corporates align with external standards that require disclosures on governance, strategy, risk management, and metrics, with a strong focus on financial materiality (e.g., impacts on revenues, costs, assets, and liabilities).

A range of frameworks shapes this reporting landscape. The Global Reporting Initiative (GRI), the most widely adopted sustainability standard, emphasizes stakeholder-driven materiality, requiring companies to capture broader sustainability impacts beyond financial outcomes. In contrast, the Sustainability Accounting Standards Board (SASB) standards—now consolidated into the International Sustainability Standards Board (ISSB)—focus on financial material, industry-specific ESG factors relevant to investors. The Task Force on Climate-related Financial Disclosures (TCFD) provides widely used guidance on climate risk governance, strategy, metrics, and scenario analysis, and its principles are embedded in ISSB's climate disclosure standard (IFRS S2). Meanwhile, the EU's Corporate Sustainability Reporting Directive (CSRD) advances reporting further by mandating double materiality, requiring companies to disclose both the financial implications of ESG risks and their broader societal and environmental impacts.

Building on these frameworks, reporting on ESG-related financial resilience typically integrates qualitative and quantitative indicators, reinforced by forward-looking scenario analysis. These frameworks extend beyond disclosure—they act as strategic tools that guide managerial decision-making, enhance adaptive capacity, and support sustainable long-term value creation.

A resilience-focused ESG disclosure generally includes the following elements:

- *Materiality and Scope*: Identify the relevant ESG factors. Apply a double materiality approach if subject to the CSRD.
- *Risk Taxonomy*: Classify risks such as climate (physical and transition), nature-related, social, and governance.
- *Scenario Design*: Develop scenarios using sources like the Network for Greening the Financial System (NGFS) and incorporate location-specific overlays from the Taskforce on Nature-related Financial Disclosures (TNFD).
- *Financial Translation*: Quantify financial impacts by linking ESG risks to price changes, volumes, cost curves, asset lives, probability of default (PD), loss given default (LGD), and liquidity metrics.
- *Results, Management Actions, and Targets*: Present ranges and sensitivities, outline mitigation strategies, and set key performance indicators (KPIs) and targets.

- *Assurance and Data Controls*: Ensure data reliability and alignment with supervisory expectations from the Basel Committee, the European Central Bank (ECB), and the Financial Stability Board (FSB).

Key metrics commonly used to measure ESG-related financial resilience—spanning both quantitative and qualitative indicators—include revenue at risk from climate transition (e.g., carbon pricing, stranded assets), energy mix dependency, renewable energy adoption, and climate-related scenario stress testing within the environmental domain; workforce turnover and resilience, supply chain disruption risk, and health and safety performance within the social domain; and board oversight of ESG risks, incidence and control of corruption, cybersecurity resilience, links to financial resilience, and cost of capital differentials (e.g., green bonds versus conventional debt) within the governance domain.

Several measurement approaches have been developed to operate these metrics. These include scenario analysis and stress testing, such as assessing portfolio performance under 1.5°C or 2°C climate pathways; risk-adjusted financial metrics, such as EBITDA-at-risk and value-at-risk models that explicitly integrate ESG factors; integrated reporting, which establishes direct links between ESG outcomes and financial statements; and impact-weighted accounting, which seeks to monetize ESG externalities and incorporate them into balance sheet representations. Influential academic contributions to these approaches include Battiston et al. (2017), Eccles et al. (2014), Khan et al. (2016), and Krueger et al. (2020).

Despite the proliferation of frameworks, methodologies, and an expanding body of scholarly research, no unified standard exists for defining or measuring ESG-related financial resilience. This gap reflects the growing importance of ESG integration into financial systems and the inherent methodological complexity involved. Data quality, consistency, and comparability challenges remain significant, while rising investor demand drives forward-looking resilience metrics based on long-term scenario analysis.

5.7 Conclusion

This chapter has demonstrated that ESG criteria are strategic assets that significantly enhance institutions' financial resilience. By synthesizing theoretical perspectives and practical insights, the discussion underscored how ESG integration enables organizations—particularly financial institutions—to better withstand, adapt to, and recover from economic, environmental, and societal disruptions. ESG factors strengthen operational continuity, reinforce investor confidence, and provide long-term strategic advantages in an increasingly volatile global economy.

The literature review highlighted that ESG and sustainable finance are deeply interconnected: ESG principles drive sustainable finance by shaping capital allocation and investor preferences, while sustainable finance reinforces the integration of ESG by aligning capital flows with responsible and resilient business practices. Global reporting frameworks developed by the ISSB, CSRD, and TCFD are central to operationalizing this relationship, providing institutions with structured approaches to assess, disclose, and manage ESG-related financial risks and opportunities.

At the same time, the chapter identified important challenges. Methodological complexity, data quality issues, and a unified standard hinder the consistent measurement and reporting of ESG-related financial resilience. These obstacles underscore the need for greater alignment among regulatory bodies, researchers, and practitioners in developing standardized metrics and robust methodologies that capture the multidimensional nature of ESG impacts.

The evidence points to ESG as a financial resilience and sustainable finance catalyst. For financial institutions, integrating ESG into strategy is no longer merely a matter of regulatory compliance or reputational management but a fundamental driver of competitiveness and long-term value creation. Future research and practice should continue to refine measurement approaches, enhance data comparability, and explore innovative ways of embedding ESG into financial decision-making, thereby advancing the dual goals of resilience and sustainability.

References

Al Azizah, U. S., & Haron, R. (2025). The sustainability imperative: Evaluating the effect of ESG on corporate financial performance before and after the pandemic. *Discover Sustainability*, *6*, 529, 1–17. https://doi.org/10.1007/s43621-025-01401-8

Ameur, H. B., & Boussetta, S. (2023). Do environmental and social practices matter for the financial resilience of companies? Evidence from US firms during the COVID-19 pandemic. *Review Quantitative Finance Accounting*, 1–35. https://doi.org/10.1007/s11156-023-01218-4

Azmi, W., Hassan, M. K., Houston, R., & Karim, M. S. (2021). ESG activities and banking performance: International evidence from emerging economies. *Journal of International Financial Markets, Institutions and Money*, *70*, 101277, 1–18. https://doi.org/10.1016/j.intfin.2020.101277

Battiston, S., Mandel, A., Monasterolo, I., Schütze, F., & Visentin, G. (2017). A climate stress-test of the financial system. *Nature Climate Change*, *7*, 283–288. https://doi.org/10.1038/nclimate3255

Broadstock, D. C., Chan, K., Cheng, L. T., & Wang, X. (2021). The role of ESG performance during times of financial crisis: Evidence from Covid in China. *Finance Research Letters*, *38*, 101716, 1–11. https://doi.org/10.1016/j.frl.2020.101716

Broto, C., & Lamas, M. (2020). Is market liquidity less resilient after the financial crisis? Evidence for US treasuries. *Economic Modelling*, *93*, 217–229. https://doi.org/10.1016/j.econmod.2020.08.001

Chang, X., Fu, K., Jin, Y., & Liem, P. F. (2022). Sustainable finance: ESG/CSR, Firm value, and investment returns. *Asia-Pacific Journal of Financial Studies*, *51*, 3, 325–371. https://doi.org/10.1111/ajfs.12379

Chen, S., Song, Y., & Gao, P. (2023). Environmental, social, and governance (ESG) performance and financial outcomes: Analyzing the impact of ESG on financial performance. *Journal of Environmental Management*, *345*, 1–15. https://doi.org/10.1016/j.jenvman.2023.118829

Data Snipper (2024). What is ESG? May 29, 2024. https://www.datasnipper.com/resources/an-introduction-to-esg?

Dauerer, A. (2025). A systematic literature review of performance measurement systems and the integration of ESG factors. *Environmental and Sustainability Indicators*, *27*, 100746, 1–18. https://doi.org/10.1016/j.indic.2025.100746

De Sousa Barbosa, A. Basilio Crispin da Silva, M. C., Bueno da Silva, L, Morioka, S. N., & Fernandes de Sousa, V. (2023). Integration of environmental, social, and governance (ESG) criteria: Their impacts on corporate sustainability performance. *Humanities and Social Sciences Communications*, *10*, 410, 1–18. https://doi.org/10.1057/s41599-023-01919-0

Doherty, R., Pérez, L., Siegel, K., & Zucher, J. (2023). *How Do ESG Goals Impact a Company's Growth Performance?* New York: McKinsey & Company. https://www.mckinsey.com/capabilities/growth-marketing-and-sales/our-insights/next-in-growth/how-do-esg-goals-impact-a-companys-growth-performance

Eccles, R. G., Ioannou, I., & Serafeim, G. (2014). The impact of corporate sustainability on organizational processes and performance. *Management Science*, *60*, 11, 2835–2857. https://doi.org/10.1287/mnsc.2014.1984

Engelhardt, N., Ekkenga, J., & Posch, P. (2021). ESG ratings and stock performance during the COVID-19 crisis. *Sustainability*, *13*, 7133, 1–15. https://doi.org/10.3390/su13137133

Gehrig, T., Iannino, M. C., & Unger, S. (2024). Social responsibility and bank resiliency. *Journal of Financial Stability*, *70*, 101191, 1–23. https://doi.org/10.1016/j.jfs.2023.101191

Hamid, F. S., Loke, Y. J., & Chin, P. N. (2023). Determinants of financial resilience: Insights from an emerging economy. *Journal of Social and Economic Development*, *25*, 479–499. https://doi.org/10.1007/s40847-023-00239-y

Kamble, P. A., Mehta, A., & Rani, N. (2025). Measuring multidimensional financial resilience: An ex-ante approach. *Social Indicators Research*, *176*, 533–567. https://doi.org/10.1007/s11205-024-03476-8

Khalil, M. A., Khalil, S., & Sinliamthong, P. (2024). From ratings to resilience: The role and implications of environmental, social, and governance (ESG) performance in corporate solvency. *Sustainable Futures*, *8*, 100304, 1–8. https://doi.org/10.1016/j.sftr.2024.100304

Khan, M., Serafeim, G., & Yoon, A. (2016). Corporate sustainability: First evidence on materiality. *Accounting Review*, *91*, 6, 1697–1724. https://doi.org/10.2308/accr-51383

Kräussl, R., Oladiran, T., & Stefanova, D. (2023). A review on ESG investing: Investors' expectations, beliefs and perceptions. *Journal of Economic Surveys*, *38*, 2, 476–502. https://doi.org/10.1111/joes.12599

Krueger, P., Sautner, Z., & Starks, L. (2020). The importance of climate risks for institutional investors. *Review of Financial Studies*, *33*, 3, 1067–1111. https://doi.org/10.1093/rfs/hhz137

Li, C., Ba, S., Ma, K., Xu, Y., Huang, W., & Huang, N. (2023). ESG rating events, financial investment behavior and corporate innovation. *Economic Analysis and Policy*, *77*, 372–387. https://doi.org/10.1016/j.eap.2022.11.013

Madgavkar, N. (2024). ESG is about how companies can create long-term, sustainable value. *CECP*. https://cecp.co/cecp-insights-blog/esg-is-about-how-companies-can-create-long-term-sustainable-value

Marsh, McLennan (2024). ESG factors are top concern for financial institutions. *Marsh*. https://www.marsh.com/en-gb/risks/climate-change-sustainability/insights/esg-factors-are-top-concern-for-financial-institutions.html

Martiny, A., Taglialatela, J., Testa, F., & Iraldo, F. (2024). Determinants of environmental social and governance (ESG) performance: A systematic literature review. *Journal of Cleaner Production*, *456*, June, 142213. https://doi.org/10.1016/j.jclepro.2024.142213

Mita, A. F., Widyawati, L., & Azhar, Z. (2024). The role of sustainability performance on financial resilience during crisis. *Business Strategy and Development*, *7* (4), e70045. https://doi.org/10.1002/bsd2.70045

MSCI (2024). The evolution of ESG investing. *MSCI*. https://www.msci.com/esg-101-what-is-esg/evolution-of-esg-investing#:~:text=The%20practice%20of%20ESG%20investing%20began%20in%20the,or%20involvement%20in%20the%20South%20African%20apartheid%20regime

Ni, K., Zhang, R., Tan, L., & Lai, X. (2024). How ESG enhances corporate competitiveness: Mechanisms and evidence, *Finance Research Letters*, *69*, 106249, 1–12. https://doi.org/10.1016/j.frl.2024.106249

Okumu, M., Ansong, D., Koomson, I., & Chen, D.-G. (2024). How financial resilience shapes social and public health policy choices in Africa: Empirical insights from the COVID-19 pandemic. *Journal of the Society for Social Work and Research*, *15* (1), 43–67. https://doi.org/10.1086/717770

Peterdy, K. (2024). ESG (Environmental, Social, & Governance). *Corporate Finance Institute*. https://corporatefinanceinstitute.com/resources/esg/esg-environmental-social-governance/

Schilirò, D. (2019). Sustainability, innovation, and efficiency: A key relationship. In M. Ziolo and B. S. Sergi (eds.), *Financing Sustainable Development*. London: Palgrave, pp. 83–102.

Schilirò, D. (2020). Sustainable public finance system. In M. Ziolo (ed.), *Finance and Sustainable Development*. London: Routledge, pp. 163–177.

Schilirò, D. (2024). Sustainable finance and sustainable public finance system, *MPRA Paper* No. 120216.

Sergi, B. S. (2024). Financial constraints and carbon emissions: An empirical investigation. *Social Responsibility Journal, 20* (4), 761–782. https://doi.org/10.1108/SRJ-01-2023-0014

Tricker, B. (2022). *The Practice of Corporate Governance*. Boca Raton (FL): CRC Press.

Ullah, S., Ullah, A., & Zaman, M. (2024). Nexus of governance, macroeconomic conditions, and financial stability of banks: a comparison of developed and emerging countries. *Financial Innovation*, *10*, 30, 1–38. https://doi.org/10.1186/s40854-023-00542-x

Van Der Vegt, G. S., Essens, P., Wahlström, M., & George, G. (2015). Managing risk and resilience. *Academy of Management Journal*, *58*, 4, 971–980. https://doi.org/10.5465/amj.2015.4004

Wang, H., Jiao, S., & Ma, C. (2024). The impact of ESG responsibility performance on corporate resilience, *International Review of Economics & Finance*, *93*, Part B, 1115–1129. https://doi.org/10.1016/j.iref.2024.05.033

Xue, H. (2025). ESG disclosure, market forces and investment efficiency. *The Accounting Review*, 1–29. https://doi.org/10.2308/tar-2023-0707

Yang, R., Caporin, M., & Jiménez-Martin, J.-A. (2024). ESG risk exposure: A tale of two tails. *Quantitative Finance*, *24*, 6, 827–849. https://doi.org/10.1080/14697688.2024.2349016

Yu, Z., Farooq, U., Alam, M. M., & Dai, J. (2024). How does environmental, social, and governance (ESG) performance determine investment mix? New empirical evidence from BRICS. *Borsa Istanbul Review*, *24* (3), 520–529. https://doi.org/10.1016/j.bir.2024.02.007

Zairis, G., Liargovas, P., & Apostolopoulos, N. (2024). Sustainable finance and ESG importance: A systematic literature review and research agenda. *Sustainability*, *16*, 7, 2878, 1–13. https://doi.org/10.3390/su16072878

Ziolo, M., Bąk, I., Cheba, K., Spoz, A., & Niedzielski, P. (2021). Sustainable financial systems toward sustainability in finance. Institutional and managerial approach. *Procedia Computer Science*, *192*, 4237–4248.

Ziolo, M., Filipiak, B. Z., Bąk, I., & Cheba, K. (2019). How to design more sustainable financial systems: The roles of environmental, social, and governance factors in the decision-making process. *Sustainability*, *11*, 20, 5604. 1–34. https://doi.org/10.3390/su11205604

Zumente, I., & Bistrova, J. (2021). ESG importance for long-term shareholder value creation: Literature vs. practice. *Journal of Open Innovation: Technology, Market, and Complexity*, *7* (2), 1–13. https://doi.org/10.3390/joitmc7020127

6 Building financial resilience

Marta Postuła and Wojciech Chmielewski

6.1 Introduction

The concept of financial resilience has undergone significant evolution in recent decades, extending beyond traditional measures of capital adequacy and liquidity management to encompass technological issues, operational continuity, and adaptive capacity in the face of multifaceted risks (IMF, 2023b). Contemporary financial institutions operate within an increasingly complex ecosystem characterized by rapid technological advancement, evolving regulatory frameworks, and unprecedented interconnectivity that can amplify both opportunities and vulnerabilities (EBA, 2023c).

Financial resilience in the modern context refers to the ability of financial institutions to absorb shocks, adapt to them, and restore operational capabilities while maintaining the continuity of critical functions and supporting the broader economy (Leitner et al., 2024). In this view, resilience is not limited to survival but includes the capacity for strengthening and adaptive evolution, arising from the assimilation of experiences gained under crisis conditions.

The contemporary landscape presents unique challenges that distinguish current resilience requirements. Digital transformation has fundamentally altered operational models, risk profiles, and stakeholder expectations while creating new vulnerabilities related to cybersecurity, data privacy, and dependencies on technology providers (FSB, 2024). The COVID-19 pandemic, geopolitical tensions, and climate-related risks have further underscored the importance of operational flexibility and scenario planning capabilities. Early warning systems have become increasingly sophisticated, integrating traditional financial indicators with alternative data sources and machine-learning algorithms to provide more comprehensive risk assessments (BIS, 2023). These systems confirm the evolution from reactive to proactive risk management, enabling institutions to identify potential vulnerabilities before they manifest as operational disruptions or financial losses. Indeed, recent research finds that

DOI: 10.4324/9781003648840-6

deploying AI-based analytical tools can significantly reduce financial risks (Cornelli et al., 2025), providing further evidence that technology adoption strengthens institutional resilience.

The regulatory landscape has similarly evolved: frameworks such as Basel III/IV, DORA, MiCA, and initiatives related to Environmental, Social, and Governance (ESG) and sustainable finance create both compliance obligations and strategic opportunities for institutions that effectively integrate these requirements into their operational models (BIS, 2023; European Commission, 2022; IMF, 2023b). This regulatory complexity requires institutions to develop advanced compliance capabilities that allow adaptation to changing requirements while maintaining operational efficiency.

6.2 Diagnosing financial resilience: Indicators and risk assessment

Measuring financial resilience requires comprehensive analytical frameworks that extend beyond traditional financial indicators to include operational, technological, and reputational dimensions. Contemporary diagnostic approaches integrate quantitative indicators with qualitative assessments, leveraging advanced analytics to obtain a complete picture of institutional vulnerabilities and adaptive capacities.

Capital adequacy indicators remain crucial for assessing resilience, with the Common Equity Tier 1 (CET1) ratio serving as a primary measure of loss absorption capacity. The Basel III frameworks introduced additional tools, such as the leverage ratio, Net Stable Funding Ratio (NSFR), and Liquidity Coverage Ratio (LCR), which provide a more comprehensive assessment of institutional stability (European Banking Authority, 2024). These indicators have been refined based on experiences from the 2007 to 2009 financial crisis, emphasizing the importance of high-quality liquid assets and stable funding sources.

Stress testing methodologies have also evolved significantly, incorporating more advanced scenario design, extended time horizons, and integration with recovery and resolution planning processes. The Comprehensive Capital Analysis and Review (CCAR) program in the United States and EU-wide tests coordinated by the European Banking Authority (EBA) exemplify how supervisory authorities use stress tests to enhance systemic resilience (EBA, 2023; Federal Reserve, 2023). In parallel, machine-learning-based methods are gaining prominence in banking literature and practice, improving predictive accuracy in forecasting defaults and credit losses. Algorithms such as gradient boosting and neural networks enhance forecast precision compared to traditional models (Jiang et al., 2023), while competing risks survival analysis models capture the dynamics of credit losses in diverse macroeconomic scenarios

(Saavedra et al., 2024). The application of these approaches promotes both regulatory compliance and the development of strategic planning capabilities (IMF, 2023a).

Technological risks are also gaining importance, requiring assessment frameworks capable of verifying cybersecurity levels, system resilience, and data management quality. The Digital Operational Resilience Act (DORA) introduces detailed requirements for Information and Communication Technology risk management, incident reporting, and third-party oversight, necessitating new assessment methodologies (European Commission, 2022; EBA, 2023). Cyber risk assessment has transformed from simple vulnerability tests to comprehensive threat modeling frameworks, encompassing analysis of attacker capabilities, attack surfaces, and the impact of potential incidents on institutional operations. Probabilistic risk quantification methods are increasingly used to better estimate potential losses and optimize defense investments (World Bank, 2020).

Climate risks remain a critical dimension, classified in the literature into two main categories: physical (e.g., floods, fires, heatwaves), leading to asset destruction and operational disruptions, and transition risks arising from the shift to a low-carbon economy (e.g., carbon taxes, environmental regulations, stranded assets). Due to their long-term nature, assessing these risks requires new methodologies capable of capturing their impact on asset values and financial institution stability. The Task Force on Climate-related Financial Disclosures (TCFD) frameworks play a key role here, providing a globally recognized approach to climate risk reporting, though practical implementation remains challenging due to limited data availability and modeling uncertainties (TCFD, 2023).

The complexity of contemporary risk landscapes necessitates integrated assessment frameworks that can evaluate interdependencies across different risk categories. Bank distress probability models have been enhanced to incorporate multiple risk factors simultaneously, providing more realistic assessments of institutional vulnerabilities (Altman et al., 2010; BCBS, 2013; IMF, 2023a). Bayesian approaches to resilience assessment offer particular opportunities for integrating diverse data sources and quantifying uncertainty in risk estimates. These methods enable institutions to continuously update risk assessments as new information emerges, enhancing both accuracy and responsiveness of evaluation processes (Chong & Klüppelberg, 2017; Rojas & Dias, 2018).

To systematize these methodological insights, Table 6.1 presents a risk alignment matrix linking key categories of financial vulnerabilities with corresponding resilience strategies.

The matrix above illustrates the strategic alignment between different risk categories and resilience management approaches. These frameworks demonstrate how institutions must adopt differentiated strategies depending

Table 6.1 Risk Alignment Matrix and Strategies for Financial Resilience

Risk Categories	*Resilience Strategies*
Capital/Liquidity	Basel III Indicators (CET1, LCR, NSFR)
Technological/Cyber	Investments in Technology and DORA
Climate (ESG)	ESG Integration and TCFD
Operational/Reputational	Business Continuity Plans and Stress Tests

Source: Authors' own elaboration.

on the nature of the risks they encounter, with particular emphasis on the importance of technology investments for managing cyber risks and ESG integration for addressing climate-related risks.

6.3 The role of regulation: Safety frameworks

Regulatory frameworks serve both as constraints and enablers of financial resilience, establishing minimum standards while providing flexibility for innovation and adaptation. The evolution of financial regulations reflects lessons learned from successive crises and represents ongoing efforts to balance stability, efficiency, and innovation in financial systems. To situate these developments temporally, Figure 6.1 summarizes key regulatory milestones since 2008.

The timeline above shows the progressive development of financial regulations from crisis response to comprehensive resilience frameworks. This evolution illustrates how regulators have shifted from reactive measures after the 2008 financial crisis to proactive frameworks that incorporate digital transformation and emerging risks. Building on this trajectory, contemporary frameworks operationalize resilience through a core set of prudential instruments.

Contemporary regulatory frameworks employ multiple instruments to enhance financial resilience, including capital requirements, liquidity standards, operational-risk management requirements, and corporate governance standards. The Basel III frameworks represent the most comprehensive international effort to strengthen banking regulation, with implementation timelines extending to 2025 to allow for gradual adjustment (European Banking Authority, 2024).

Capital requirements have been refined to better capture potential threats while providing appropriate incentives for prudent institutional management. The introduction of capital buffers—including conservation, countercyclical, and systemic importance buffers—enables supervisors to flexibly adjust requirements based on economic conditions and systemic stability assessments (BCBS, 2019; BIS, 2017). Liquidity regulations, comprehensively introduced under Basel III, mandate institutions

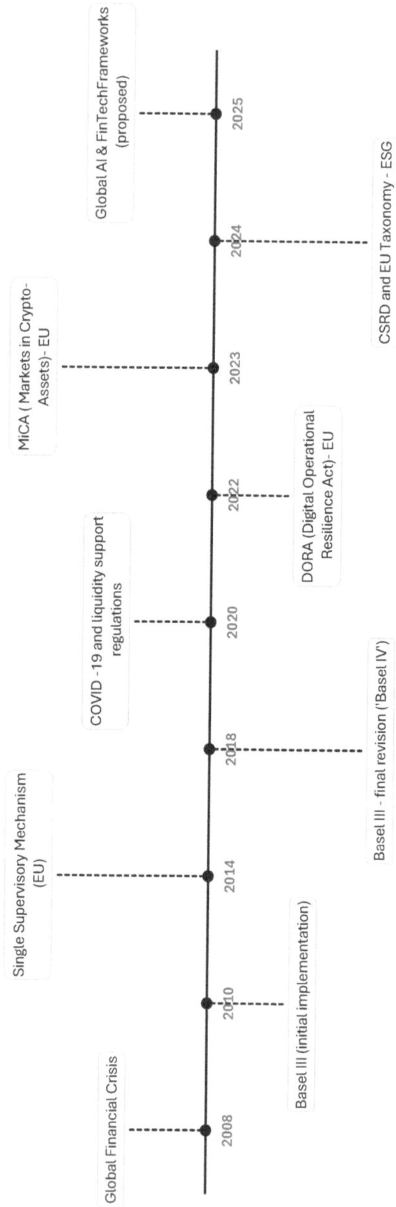

Figure 6.1 Evolution of financial regulations: Key milestones 2008–2025.

Source: Authors' own elaboration.

to maintain adequate pools of high-quality liquid assets to survive funding crisis scenarios. The LCR and NSFR cover different time horizons and funding structure aspects, providing complementary perspectives on liquidity adequacy (EBA, 2023).

While these tools are broadly shared, their calibration and enforcement vary markedly across jurisdictions, warranting a comparative perspective. The implementation of international regulatory standards varies significantly by geographic region, reflecting different regulatory philosophies, market structures, and policy priorities. Comparative analysis reveals three distinct models: the market-oriented approach in the United States, the harmonized and ESG-focused approach in the European Union, and the state-controlled approach in China.

The US regulatory framework emphasizes market discipline and regulatory flexibility, with multiple federal agencies sharing supervisory responsibilities. The Federal Reserve's approach to banking supervision combines rigorous stress testing with principles-based guidance, granting institutions significant flexibility in implementation (Federal Reserve, 2023). This approach reflects confidence in market mechanisms for efficient capital allocation while maintaining oversight of systemic threats. Recent changes include increased focus on operational resilience, particularly in cybersecurity and third-party management (Federal Reserve, 2020; BCBS, 2021).

By contrast, the European Union pursues a harmonized, rules-based regime that embeds sustainability into prudential policy. In practice, this is operationalized through the EU Taxonomy, Corporate Sustainability Reporting Directive, and Sustainable Finance Disclosure Regulation, alongside DORA's digital operational resilience framework. The European Banking Authority coordinates the implementation of EU standards, allowing some national discretion in specific areas (EBA, 2024). European regulations are characterized by comprehensive frameworks addressing multiple aspects of financial institution operations. The DORA establishes detailed requirements for digital operational resilience, covering cybersecurity, ICT management, and third-party relationships (European Commission, 2022). ESG integration is a distinguishing feature of European regulations, with the EU Taxonomy, CSRD Directive, and SFDR Regulation creating comprehensive frameworks for sustainable risk management and disclosure (European Commission, 2022, 2023b).

A third, state-centric model is exemplified by China, where supervisory objectives are closely coupled with industrial policy and macro-stability goals. China's regulatory approach reflects the structure of its financial system, where state ownership dominance in major institutions enables direct government intervention in supervisory and credit processes (IMF, 2025). Until 2023, comprehensive oversight of the banking and insurance sector was exercised by the China Banking and Insurance Regulatory Commission (CBIRC), whose competencies were subsequently assumed by the newly established National Financial Regulatory Administration (NFRA) (State Council of the PRC, 2023). Chinese supervision extends beyond prudential regulations to strategic and operational objectives. Recent changes focus on strengthening control over the fintech sector and activities of large technology firms, reflecting concerns about market concentration and systemic threats (BIS, 2023).

Amid rising regulatory complexity and reporting intensity across jurisdictions, traditional compliance functions are increasingly strained, accelerating the adoption of regulatory technology (RegTech). Harnessing digital innovations, RegTech streamlines supervisory and reporting processes—shifting oversight from periodic, manual checks to continuous, data-driven monitoring—and thereby reduces the cost of meeting regulatory requirements (Arner et al., 2017; Zetzsche et al., 2020). These technologies support real-time reporting, automation of reporting processes, and predictive analysis of potential irregularities. Regulatory sandboxes are also important tools, allowing testing of new technologies and business models under controlled conditions, ensuring a balance between innovation and oversight (Zetzsche et al., 2020). These initiatives demonstrate that regulators are beginning to view digital innovations not only as challenges but also as tools for strengthening financial system resilience.

RegTech forms part of a broader technological turn in finance, in which digital tools both extend efficiency frontiers and reshape the risk landscape. Digital transformation has created opportunities to enhance efficiency and service quality, but it has also introduced new classes of threats. Recognizing and managing this duality—technology as an enabler of stability and a source of systemic risk—is essential for designing coherent resilience strategies.

Within this technological turn, artificial intelligence (AI) and machine learning (ML) exemplify how digital tools extend analytical frontiers: they enable advanced pattern recognition, predictive modelling, and automated decision-making, allowing institutions to process large data streams in real time and to surface threats and opportunities that remain invisible to traditional methods (Jiang et al., 2023; OECD, 2024). Beyond AI/ML, distributed-ledger technologies can bolster operational resilience by increasing transparency, lowering settlement risk, and reducing dependence on intermediaries; smart contracts automate complex workflows, thereby curbing operational risk and improving auditability. Yet constraints related to scalability, energy use, and regulatory uncertainty limit near-term deployment at scale (Catalini & Gans, 2020; World Bank, 2019).

Complementing these analytics and transaction-layer tools, cloud platforms provide elastic capacity and geographic redundancy that support continuity of critical operations under stress. The ability to scale resources rapidly and to draw on distributed infrastructure can enhance uptime, although concentration among a small set of providers introduces system-level vulnerabilities that require active oversight (EBA, 2021). In parallel, RegTech leverages the same digital stack to automate monitoring, reporting, and anomaly detection, lowering compliance costs while improving the timeliness and accuracy of supervisory data and enabling more proactive identification of issues.

Notwithstanding these gains, digitalization expands the attack surface. The rising sophistication and frequency of cyber incidents call for continuous investment in defense-in-depth and rehearsed incident-response capabilities, as the consequences extend beyond direct financial loss to reputational damage, regulatory sanctions, and persistent operational disruption (ENISA, 2024; Kopp et al., 2017).

These dynamics are mirrored in recent sectoral data: Figure 6.2 juxtaposes the post-2021 moderation in fintech investment with a continued rise in reported cyber incidents across financial services, underscoring that innovation cycles have not been matched by commensurate improvements in security posture.

The divergent trends in Figure 6.3 highlight a persistent tension in the fintech ecosystem: while investment volumes receded from their 2021 peak, reported cybersecurity incidents continued to rise, indicating that the security posture has not kept pace with innovation. This divergence underscores the need to calibrate technological expansion with proportionate investment in protection and response capabilities.

Within this heightened threat environment, ransomware stands out as a particularly destabilizing vector. Such attacks can paralyze core operations, with restoration of access to critical systems often contingent on meeting the attackers' demands. Given the dense interconnections within financial networks, the impact frequently propagates beyond the initially affected firm, creating the potential for systemic spillovers. These characteristics make coordinated action—between private institutions and public authorities—an essential component of sectoral defense.

Compounding these pressures are structural concentration risks associated with data centralization. The shift toward public cloud, specialized data centers, and external technology platforms delivers scale and efficiency, yet simultaneously creates single points of failure. A breach or prolonged outage at one critical node can transmit widely across institutions that share the same infrastructure layer, magnifying operational risk.

These concentration dynamics are further amplified by the complexity of third-party ecosystems. As financial institutions deepen reliance on cloud providers and niche technology vendors, their operational resilience becomes inseparable from that of their suppliers. Robust third-party risk management—encompassing rigorous due diligence, continuous performance and security monitoring, and pre-arranged contingency and exit plans—thus becomes a direct prerequisite for institutional continuity.

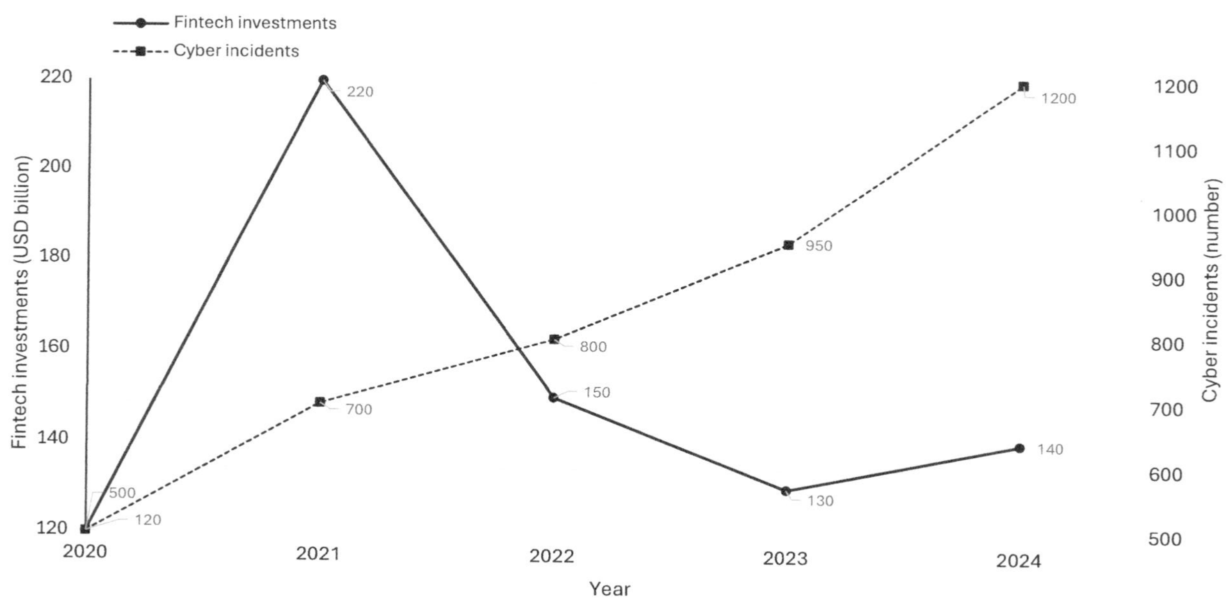

Figure 6.2 Fintech investments and cybersecurity incidents in financial services (2020–2024).

Source: Authors' own elaboration based on data from KPMG (2023), CB Insights (2023), ENISA (2024), and FS-ISAC (2023).

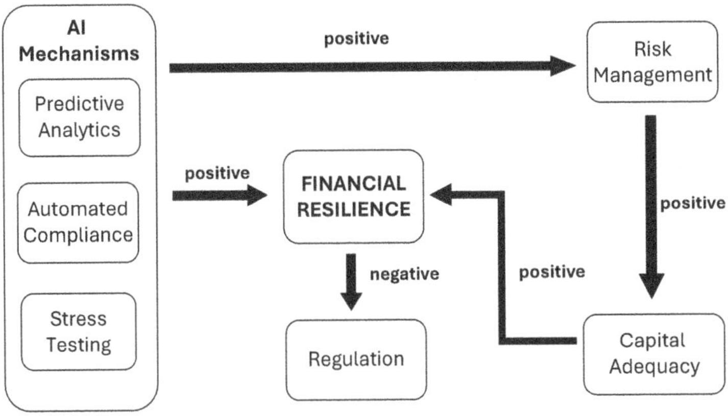

Figure 6.3 Conceptual framework of AI's influence on institutional financial resilience.

Source: Authors' own elaboration based on Liu et al. (2025), Financial Stability Board (2024), and Beereddy and Kumar (2022).

6.4 Fintech and business models: Innovation and risk in resilience

The development of financial technology firms and the implementation of innovative fintech solutions by traditional financial institutions have fundamentally transformed the financial services landscape. These changes have created new opportunities in efficiency and innovation while introducing new risks and altering competitive dynamics in the sector.

In the payments area, fintechs have played a particular role, improving accessibility, efficiency, and user experience. Digital payment platforms have contributed to reducing transaction costs and shortening settlement times while enabling expanded access to financial services for underserved social groups. Mobile banking applications have changed customer expectations and introduced new service delivery models that can operate at lower costs than traditional branch networks (PwC, 2022).

A similar transformation is evident in lending. Alternative lending platforms use advanced analytics and alternative data sources to extend credit to borrowers who would not meet traditional creditworthiness assessment requirements. This enables them to process loan applications faster and at lower costs while—thanks to more advanced risk models—achieving results comparable to or better than traditional lenders (EY, 2023).

Significant innovations have also encompassed investment services. Robo-advisory platforms have increased access to wealth management services, offering automated investment portfolios based on modern portfolio theory and algorithmic rebalancing, at significantly lower costs than traditional wealth management services. These solutions have enabled a broader audience to access investment tools beyond high-net-worth clients (Deloitte, 2023; KPMG, 2024b).

All these models rely heavily on intensive data utilization. The implementation of big data analytics enables fintechs to develop more advanced risk assessment methods and deeper understanding of customer preferences, exceeding the capabilities of traditional institutions that still rely primarily on structured financial data. Alternative information sources, such as social media activity, transaction patterns, or behavioral analytics, allow for creating a fuller picture of creditworthiness and consumer behaviors (KPMG, 2024a).

Despite numerous innovations, fintech firms often operate based on business models that may be less resilient than traditional financial institutions. Many operate with minimal capital buffers, relying primarily on external funding and rapid revenue growth rather than building significant reserves to survive adverse market conditions (BIS, 2023).

Technological dependencies are also a significant area of vulnerability. Fintechs base their operations largely on digital platforms and external service providers, exposing them to operational risk. Unlike traditional financial institutions, which have more diversified distribution channels and manual processes, many fintechs have limited capabilities to operate in the event of failures in their primary technology systems.

Regulatory uncertainty must also be counted among risk factors. The rapid pace of innovation in the sector often outpaces the development of adequate regulations, leading to situations where supervisory requirements remain unclear or subject to frequent changes. Such uncertainty hinders business planning, limits capital-raising opportunities, and complicates long-term strategic development.

Another challenge is the high costs of customer acquisition and retention. To maintain a competitive position, fintech firms must continuously invest in marketing and product development. At the same time, low switching costs, which are a significant advantage for consumers, make customers easily migrate to competitors. As a result, many fintechs struggle with unstable customer bases, further increasing operational risks.

Differences in regulatory approaches to fintechs in the United States, the European Union, and China reflect distinct priorities in balancing innovation and stability, with significant implications for both sector development and financial system stability.

In the United States, regulations focus primarily on consumer protection and limiting systemic risk while leaving space for market-driven and funded innovations. The fragmented regulatory framework involves actions by multiple federal agencies, including the Securities and Exchange Commission (SEC), Commodity Futures Trading Commission (CFTC), and Consumer Financial Protection Bureau (CFPB). At the same time, individual states introduce their own supervisory regulations, causing fintechs to often be subject to oversight by multiple institutions (Zetzsche et al., 2020). Programs such as the "Innovation Office" at the OCC or state-level regulatory sandboxes (e.g., in Arizona) allow testing of new business models under limited supervision (US Treasury, 2022).

In the European Union, the regulatory approach is more harmonized and based on comprehensive legal frameworks that ensure uniform standards across the Community. The Payment Services Directive (PSD2) introduced open banking principles, increasing competition in the payment services market and enabling the development of innovative business models. Data protection, based on the General Data Protection Regulation (GDPR), has significantly influenced fintech operations, requiring explicit consent for data processing and strengthening consumer rights (European Commission, 2018). New regulations, such as the Markets in Crypto-Assets Regulation (MiCA) and the DORA, further emphasize the EU's commitment to integrating technological innovations with financial security and stability (ECB, 2022).

China's regulatory approach has evolved from initial tolerance for rapid innovation development to increasingly centralized and restrictive oversight. The CBIRC and the People's Bank of China (PBoC) exercise broad supervision over the sector, encompassing both financial stability and economic policy objectives. Regulations concerning entities such as Ant Group or Tencent introduced after 2020 reflect concerns about systemic risk and market concentration (PBoC, 2021). At the same time, the development of the national digital currency (e-CNY) shows that regulations are treated not only as a supervisory tool but also as a mechanism supporting political goals, such as financial inclusion and technological sovereignty (Allen et al., 2022).

Empirical research increasingly confirms that AI exerts a significantly positive effect on the financial resilience of institutions. Liu et al. (2025) demonstrate that AI adoption leads to a substantial reduction in corporate financial risk through three principal channels—structural, resource-based, and technological—particularly in non-high-tech firms and industries characterized by lower uncertainty (Liu et al., 2025).

In the context of Basel III capital requirements, Beereddy and Kumar (2022) show that machine-learning techniques such as XGBoost and neural networks achieve superior predictive accuracy compared to traditional models when estimating regulatory capital needs, resulting in improved capital adequacy ratios. Moreover, the Financial Stability Board emphasizes that AI enhances operational efficiency, regulatory compliance, and advanced data analytics, all of which are critical for reinforcing financial resilience (Financial Stability Board, 2024).

Notably, AI's application in stress testing enables the generation of more dynamic and sensitive shock scenarios than conventional historical models, thereby allowing financial institutions to predict capital and liquidity pressures with greater precision and, in turn, bolster their resilience (Beereddy & Kumar, 2022; Fonton Moffo, 2024).

6.5 Strategies for building resilience

Building financial resilience today requires a multidimensional approach. In practice, effectiveness hinges on integrating traditional financial management with modern technologies, advanced operational-risk frameworks, and planning processes that allow flexible responses to changing economic and regulatory conditions. Before turning to specific levers, Figure 6.3 maps the principal channels through which AI shapes institutional resilience and situates technology alongside balance-sheet and organizational foundations.

The diagram illustrates the multi-channel pathways through which AI affects institutional financial resilience. AI exerts a primarily positive influence via predictive analytics that support risk management, automation of compliance processes, and advanced stress-scenario testing. At the same time, these technologies can generate additional regulatory challenges, necessitating a holistic approach to governing both the benefits and the risks associated with AI adoption. Empirical studies indicate that, when properly implemented, AI materially strengthens all core pillars of institutional financial resilience.

While technology increasingly mediates resilience outcomes, effectiveness remains anchored in balance-sheet strength; accordingly, the foundation of financial resilience lies in rigorous capital and liquidity management. Adequate loss-absorbing capital sustains stakeholder confidence under stress, and contemporary capital strategies aim not merely to satisfy regulatory minima but to reconcile prudential requirements with business objectives and stakeholder expectations. Dynamic capital planning, informed by supervisory stress-test results and applicable regulations, supports the optimal allocation of resources across business lines and risk categories. Experience from the global financial crisis, together with the implementation of Basel III, has reinforced the centrality of liquidity requirements: institutions maintain high-quality liquid assets, manage funding costs, and cultivate durable market relationships. Liquidity planning is increasingly integrated with strategic planning to enable rapid responses to shocks, while recovery and resolution planning reduces the risk of disorderly failure by identifying critical functions and pre-defining restructuring options.

Buffers alone are insufficient; translating balance-sheet capacity into durable stability requires robust risk-management architectures and rehearsed continuity arrangements. Accordingly, resilience hinges on frameworks that integrate financial, operational, technological, and strategic risks (BCBS, 2021). The growing use of loss-event databases and forward-looking assessments enables proactive intervention rather than ex post crisis response. Lessons from the COVID-19 shock underscored the value of pre-tested continuity plans capable of sustaining critical functions under severe disruption. The rapid scaling of remote work, digital service channels, and alternative procedures expanded organizational flexibility and response capacity. To align these elements, formal crisis-management playbooks—defining escalation paths, decision rights, and communications—have become a core pillar of resilience.

These organizational capabilities are increasingly data-enabled. Digital technologies—AI in particular—have become, alongside capital and liquidity, a co-determinant of resilience because they expand analytical capacity and introduce new decision and attack vectors. In practice, AI is deployed for fraud detection, credit-risk assessment, liquidity monitoring, support to stress testing, and market surveillance; supervisory reviews report higher accuracies and shorter response times, which can translate into lower operational and credit losses (FSB, 2024; IOSCO, 2025; Leitner et al., 2024). Empirical evidence likewise indicates that machine-learning techniques outperform classical models (e.g., logistic regression): in a cross-sectional credit-scoring benchmark, ensemble and deep algorithms achieved higher area-under-the-ROC-curve (AUC) scores, yielding fewer misclassifications, more accurate risk pricing, and better capital allocation (Lessmann et al., 2015). These performance gains are contingent rather than automatic and depend on disciplined model-risk management (independent validation, backtesting, and drift monitoring) and sound data governance; without such safeguards, vulnerabilities emerge in the form of model opacity and bias, procyclical decision herding, and operational concentration (FSB, 2024; BIS–FSI, 2024; Leitner et al., 2024). Guidance therefore emphasizes explainability (XAI), a human-in-the-loop principle for high-materiality decisions, supplier due diligence, and credible exit plans (IOSCO, 2025; EBA, 2021).

Beyond classical AI, an adjacent technological frontier—quantum computing—presents a distinct combination of risks and opportunities for resilience. On the threat side, advances in quantum computation undermine widely used asymmetric cryptography and enable "harvest-now, decrypt-later" strategies, which make migration to post-quantum cryptography (PQC) and quantum-safe communication channels urgent (BIS Innovation Hub, 2023; NIST, 2024). On the opportunity side, the literature documents speed-ups in Monte Carlo simulation and in the estimation of risk measures (e.g., VaR/CVaR) via quantum amplitude estimation, enabling denser and more accurate intra-day scenario analysis and more responsive portfolio optimization (Montanaro, 2015; Woerner & Egger, 2019). In operational terms, a dual-track approach is implied: simultaneously hardening cryptography (inventory, crypto-agility, migration testing) and conducting controlled pilots that leverage quantum advantages in risk and optimization, so that technology functions as a net amplifier of resilience rather than a new source of fragility.

Table 6.2 synthesizes the discussion by comparing AI/ML and quantum technologies across six dimensions—role in resilience, applications,

Table 6.2 Digital and Quantum Technologies and Financial Resilience: Comparative Overview

Section	*AI/ML*	*Quantum Technologies*
Role in resilience	Expanded analytical capacity and faster response; simultaneously introduces new decision and attack vectors (FSB, 2024).	Potential to strengthen security via PQC and to accelerate compute-heavy analytics, while introducing cryptographic transition exposures (NIST, 2024; BIS Innovation Hub, 2023).
Applications	Fraud detection; credit scoring; liquidity monitoring; stress testing; market surveillance (FSB, 2024; ECB, 2024; IOSCO, 2025).	Accelerated Monte Carlo and VaR/CVaR estimation (QAE); portfolio optimisation; quantum-safe communications (PQC/QKD) (Montanaro, 2015; Woerner & Egger, 2019; NIST, 2024).
Effects (conditional)	Higher AUC and shorter reaction times → fewer decision errors, improved risk pricing and capital allocation (Lessmann et al., 2015; FSB, 2024).	Denser/cheaper scenario analysis and faster optimisation—subject to hardware/algorithm maturity (Montanaro, 2015; Woerner & Egger, 2019).
Conditions (enablers)	Model risk management (independent validation, backtesting, drift monitoring); XAI and human-in-the-loop; strong data governance and vendor management (IOSCO, 2025; Rudin, 2019; EBA, 2021).	Crypto-agility and cryptography inventory; pilots/sandboxes; interoperability and side-channel testing; provider due diligence and exit plans (NIST, 2024; ENISA, 2023; BIS Innovation Hub, 2023).
Risks	Opacity/bias and decision herding; dependency on a few cloud/model providers and operational concentration (FSB, 2024; BCBS, 2022).	Harvest-now-decrypt-later; migration/coexistence errors; hardware/algorithm immaturity; concentration among "quantum cloud" providers (NIST, 2024; ENISA, 2023; BCBS, 2022).

(*Continued*)

Table 6.2 (Continued)

Section	*AI/ML*	*Quantum Technologies*
Institutional response	AI/ML programme: XAI, human-in-the-loop, MRM, data governance; supplier due diligence and exit plans (IOSCO, 2025; BCBS, 2022).	Quantum programme: PQC migration plan (inventory → crypto-agility → migration testing); pilots for QAE/ Monte Carlo/portfolio optimisation (NIST, 2024; BIS Innovation Hub, 2023).

Selected sources: BCBS (2022); BIS Innovation Hub, 2023; ECB (2024); ENISA (2023); FSB (2024); IOSCO (2025); Lessmann et al. (2015); Montanaro (2015); NIST (2024); Woerner & Egger (2019); Rudin (2019); EBA (2021).

Notes: AUC — area under the ROC curve; MRM — model risk management; PQC — post-quantum cryptography; QAE — quantum amplitude estimation; QKD — quantum key distribution.

conditional effects, enabling conditions, risks, and institutional responses—thereby distilling their practical and prudential implications.

Both balance-sheet and technological levers operate within a broader institutional context shaped by ESG considerations and an evolving compliance architecture, which can amplify or attenuate the effects outlined above. ESG integration has become not only a regulatory expectation but also a strategic mechanism for aligning risk management with stakeholder demands. Climate-scenario analysis and stress testing inform assessments of how environmental change may affect assets and operations, while social and governance dimensions—responsible customer treatment, workforce practices, and board oversight—reinforce organizational legitimacy. The implementation of frameworks such as Basel III/IV, DORA, MiCA, and CSRD demonstrates that regulatory compliance, when embedded in processes and information systems, can function as a resilience multiplier rather than a purely administrative cost.

6.6 Comparative analysis of resilience models: United States, EU, and China

In analyzing financial resilience, one cannot overlook the diverse regulatory approaches that shape institutional practices in different parts of the world. In particular, the United States, the European Union, and China represent three distinct models—from market-oriented, through harmonized and strongly ESG-linked to state-oriented and subordinated to strategic goals. Comparing them from one perspective allows capturing fundamental differences in supervisory philosophy, institutional structure, and political priorities.

Table 6.3 Comparative Analysis of Regulatory Approaches to Financial Resilience: USA, EU, and China

Aspect	*United States*	*European Union*	*China*
Regulatory Philosophy	Market-oriented, principles-based, emphasis on flexibility and market discipline	Harmonized, rules-based, strong ESG integration	State-controlled, directive, aligned with national policy goals
Key Supervisory Bodies	Federal Reserve, OCC, FDIC, SEC, CFPB (fragmented)	ECB (SSM), EBA, ESMA (centralized at EU level)	NFRA, PBoC, CSRC (centralized under state control)
Capital and Liquidity Focus	CCAR/DFAST stress tests, tailored requirements	Basel III/IV, CRR/CRD, harmonized across members	Basel-compliant but with state-directed adjustments
Digital Resilience	Guidance on cybersecurity and third-party risks	DORA, comprehensive ICT and cyber requirements	Strict fintech controls, e-CNY for digital oversight
ESG Integration	Emerging focus, voluntary TCFD adoption	EU Taxonomy, CSRD, SFDR mandatory	Green finance aligned with national development plans
Innovation Approach	Regulatory sandboxes at state level, innovation offices	PSD2 open banking, MiCA for crypto	Controlled innovation, focus on financial inclusion
Systemic Risk Management	Emphasis on SIFIs, resolution planning	SSM for cross-border supervision	Direct intervention in large entities

Source: Authors' own elaboration based on regulatory frameworks in the USA, EU, and China.

Table 6.3 presents a comparison of these three approaches, indicating both common elements and specific features that influence the way financial resilience is built in individual jurisdictions.

The comparative analysis presented above reveals fundamental differences in the approach to financial resilience across the three major regulatory jurisdictions. These differences reflect not only varying regulatory philosophies but also distinct economic systems, market structures, and political priorities.

In the United States, the approach to financial resilience is characterized by emphasis on market discipline, regulatory flexibility, and institution-specific solutions rather than prescriptive requirements uniform across the sector. These mechanisms reflect confidence in the market's role in efficient capital allocation and in institutional management's development of risk management capabilities. A key supervisory tool is stress testing, including the CCAR and Dodd-Frank Act Stress Tests (DFAST), conducted by the Federal Reserve. These exercises combine quantitative analysis with qualitative assessment of risk management practices, enabling identification of vulnerabilities while preserving institutional flexibility in remedial actions (Federal Reserve, 2023). The principles-based regulatory approach provides institutions with significant leeway in implementing regulatory requirements, provided they achieve intended supervisory objectives. The fragmentation of the US supervisory system—including the Fed, OCC, FDIC, SEC, and state authorities—increases compliance complexity but simultaneously enables regulatory competition and fosters innovation (Allen et al., 2022).

In the European Union, the approach to financial resilience focuses on harmonization across member states and integration of ESG factors into prudential frameworks. The Single Supervisory Mechanism (SSM) plays a crucial role, ensuring uniform oversight of the largest eurozone banks and enabling consistent application of regulatory standards, limiting regulatory arbitrage. ECB-SSM supervisory priorities include resilience assessment, forward-looking supervision, and ESG integration into risk evaluation processes (European Central Bank, 2022). The Digital Operational Resilience Act (DORA) establishes detailed digital resilience requirements, covering cybersecurity, ICT management, and third-party risks (European Commission, 2022). Additionally, the EU Taxonomy, CSRD, and SFDR create comprehensive frameworks for sustainable finance, strengthening European leadership in this area (EBA, 2023).

In China, the approach to financial resilience reflects the system's structure, where state-owned institutions dominate, enabling direct government intervention in strategies and operations. In 2023, the National Administration of Financial Regulation (NAFR) was established, assuming CBIRC competencies and serving as the overarching regulator for the banking and insurance sector (State Council of the People's Republic of China, 2023). Fintech regulations in China have shifted from initial tolerance to more rigorous oversight, exemplified by intervention in Ant Group, reflecting concerns about systemic risk and market concentration. Parallel development of the e-CNY provides the People's Bank of China with direct control over digital payments and serves as a tool for enhancing sector oversight (People's Bank of China, 2022).

Despite differing regulatory philosophies, certain areas of convergence are evident, particularly in operational resilience, cybersecurity, and third-party risk management. International organizations such as the Basel Committee on Banking Supervision, Financial Stability Board, and IOSCO support standard harmonization in these areas (BCBS, 2023; FSB, 2022). However, clear differences persist regarding the state's role, balance between innovation and stability, and integration of non-financial policy goals into regulations. These divergences arise from distinct economic and political structures and will persist in the foreseeable future.

The presented comparative analysis emphasizes that despite common challenges—such as cybersecurity, technological risks, or ESG integration—the paths to building resilience in the United States, EU, and China remain distinct. This differentiation has several implications for the global financial system. First, regulatory fragmentation hinders cross-border institutions from implementing consistent strategies, forcing adaptation to multi-layered and often conflicting requirements (FSB, 2022). Second, the risk of regulatory arbitrage increases, where entities may shift operations to jurisdictions offering more flexible regulatory solutions (BCBS, 2023). Third, different models create varying conditions for innovation—the US approach fosters rapid fintech development, the European focuses on regulatory compliance and ESG, and the Chinese links finance to industrial policy (IMF, 2023b). Finally, these divergences limit full regulatory convergence possibilities but strengthen the importance of international organizations in coordinating standards for stability and resilience (IOSCO, 2023).

6.7 Recommendations for financial institutions

The analysis presented in this chapter shows that financial resilience in the contemporary environment requires a multidimensional approach that integrates traditional prudential measures with new technological capabilities, comprehensive risk management frameworks, and forward-looking regulatory compliance strategies. It cannot be adequately assessed or strengthened using a single indicator or approach, as it encompasses various dimensions—from capital and liquidity adequacy, through operational continuity and technological resilience, to regulatory compliance and strategic adaptive capacity. Institutions that develop only in selected areas, neglecting others, may prove vulnerable to unexpected shocks or changing conditions.

Thus, the key is the evolution of risk management approaches—from reactive responses to disruptions toward proactive anticipation and preparation for potential challenges. In practice, this means investing in analytical capabilities, scenario planning, and stress testing that allow identifying weaknesses before they transform into operational or financial problems. In this context, ESG factor integration plays an increasingly important role, reflecting both regulatory requirements and stakeholder expectations extending beyond traditional financial performance measures. Institutions effectively combining environmental, social, and governance aspects with risk management and strategic planning processes achieve greater long-term resilience while better responding to growing regulatory and societal demands.

Increasingly, AI and digital infrastructure shape financial resilience. AI technologies can significantly enhance financial institution capabilities but simultaneously create new risks that current regulatory frameworks may not fully capture. Concentration of computing capabilities in large-scale data centers, or so-called AI gigafactories, may lead to systemic vulnerabilities requiring new supervisory mechanisms. Challenges also remain in managing AI-based systems, particularly regarding algorithmic transparency, bias avoidance, and ensuring appropriate human oversight. Institutions must thus balance automation benefits with the need for accountability and control.

Investments in digital infrastructure have become essential for maintaining competitiveness and operational resilience, yet they require simultaneous strengthening of cybersecurity, data protection, and third-party risk management. Experiences from the COVID-19 pandemic have highlighted the critical importance of digital capabilities for business continuity while revealing vulnerabilities that can be exploited by malicious actors. This confirms that financial resilience must be treated as a dynamic process encompassing integration of traditional stability foundations with modern technologies, ESG strategies, and systemic risk management approaches under uncertainty and rapid change.

Based on the analysis presented in this chapter, several strategic recommendations emerge for financial institutions seeking to strengthen their resilience:

- Develop Integrated Resilience Frameworks: Institutions should develop comprehensive frameworks that integrate capital and liquidity management, operational-risk management, technological capabilities, and regulatory compliance into coherent strategic approaches. These frameworks should account for interdependencies between different risk categories and enable coordinated responses to adverse events.
- Invest in Digital Capabilities: Institutions must continue investing in digital infrastructure, cybersecurity, and data analytics capabilities while carefully managing associated risks. This includes developing internal capabilities where appropriate, while maintaining effective oversight of external providers and technological dependencies.
- Enhance Scenario Planning and Stress Testing: Institutions should develop advanced scenario planning and stress testing capabilities that can assess resilience under various adverse conditions, while identifying potential vulnerabilities and mitigation strategies. These capabilities should encompass traditional financial risks as well as operational, technological, and strategic risks.
- Integrate ESG Factors: Environmental, social, and governance factors should be integrated into risk management frameworks, strategic planning processes, and performance measurement systems. This integration

should address both regulatory requirements and stakeholder expectations, while recognizing potential sources of competitive advantage.

- Strengthen Third-Party Risk Management: As institutions increasingly rely on technology providers, cloud vendors, and other external service providers, comprehensive third-party risk management capabilities become essential for maintaining operational resilience. This includes due diligence, continuous monitoring, and contingency planning for critical service provider relationships.
- Develop Adaptive Governance Structures: Governance structures must be capable of adapting to changing conditions while maintaining effective oversight and accountability. This includes board and management capabilities to oversee emerging risks, evaluate strategic options, and ensure appropriate resource allocation for resilience building.
- Foster Innovation While Managing Risk: Institutions must balance innovation with risk management, developing capabilities to assess new technologies and business models while maintaining appropriate risk controls. This includes establishing innovation frameworks, participating in regulatory sandboxes, and strategic partnerships that enable controlled experimentation with new approaches.

The path forward requires recognition that building resilience is an ongoing process, not a destination, and institutions must continually adapt their capabilities as conditions evolve. Integrating traditional financial management practices with new technologies, comprehensive risk management frameworks, and forward-looking regulatory compliance strategies forms the foundation for enhanced resilience in an increasingly complex and dynamic environment. Success in building financial resilience will require sustained leadership commitment, appropriate resource allocation, and cultural changes that embed resilience thinking across all aspects of institutional operations. Institutions that achieve such integration will be better positioned to navigate future challenges while supporting economic growth and stability.

References

Allen, F., Gu, X., & Jagtiani, J. (2022). Fintech, cryptocurrencies, and CBDC: Financial structural transformation in China. *Journal of International Money and Finance*, *124*, 102625. https://doi.org/10.1016/j.jimonfin.2022.102625.

Altman, E. I., Sabato, G., & Wilson, N. (2010). The value of non-financial information in small and medium-sized enterprise risk management. *Journal of Credit Risk*, *6*(2), 95–127. https://doi.org/10.21314/JCR.2010.110

Arner, D. W., Barberis, J., & Buckley, R. P. (2017). Fintech, RegTech and the reconceptualization of financial regulation. *Northwestern Journal of International Law & Business*, *37*(3), 371–413.

Bank for International Settlements. (2017). *Basel III: Finalising post-crisis reforms*. https://www.bis.org/bcbs/publ/d424.htm

Bank for International Settlements. (2023). *Making China's financial system better serve the real economy* (BIS Papers No. 148). https://www.bis.org/publ/bppdf/bispap148_e.pdf

Bank for International Settlements, Financial Stability Institute. (2024). *Regulating AI in the financial sector: Recent developments and main challenges* (FSI Insights No. 63). https://www.bis.org/fsi/publ/insights63.pdf

Bank for International Settlements, Innovation Hub. (2023). *Project Leap: Quantum-safe communication for the financial sector*. https://www.bis.org/publ/othp67.pdf

Basel Committee on Banking Supervision. (2013). *Principles for effective risk data aggregation and risk reporting (BCBS 239)*. https://www.bis.org/publ/bcbs239.pdf

Basel Committee on Banking Supervision. (2019). *Basel III monitoring report*. https://www.bis.org/bcbs/publ/d477.pdf

Basel Committee on Banking Supervision. (2021). *Principles for operational resilience*. https://www.bis.org/bcbs/publ/d516.htm

Basel Committee on Banking Supervision. (2023). Basel Committee work programme 2023–24. *Bank for International Settlements*. https://www.bis.org/bcbs/publ/d539.htm

Beereddy, S. R., & Kumar, K. K. (2022). Enhancing capital adequacy in banks using AI and machine learning. *Journal of Computational Analysis and Applications*, *30*(2), 549–573. https://eudoxuspress.com/index.php/pub/article/view/2906

Catalini, C., & Gans, J. S. (2020). Some simple economics of the blockchain. *Communications of the ACM*, *63*(7), 80–90. https://doi.org/10.1145/3359552

CB Insights. (2023). *State of fintech 2023 report*. https://www.cbinsights.com/research/report/fintech-trends-2023/

Chong, W., & Klüppelberg, C. (2017). Contagion in financial systems: A Bayesian network approach. *SIAM Journal on Financial Mathematics* *9*(1), 28–53. https://doi.org/10.1137/17M1116659

Cornelli, G., Gambacorta, L., Garratt, R., & Reghezza, A. (2025). Why DeFi lending? Evidence from Aave V2. *Journal of Financial Intermediation*, *63*, Article 101166. https://doi.org/10.1016/j.jfi.2025.101166

Deloitte. (2023). *Digital investment management outlook*. https://www.deloitte.com/content/dam/insights/articles/2024/us175546_cfs_fsi-outlook-investment-mgmt/di-us175546-cfs-fsi-outlook-investment-mgmt.pdf

European Banking Authority. (2021). Report on the use of digital platforms in the EU banking and payments sector. *European Banking Authority*.

https://www.eba.europa.eu/sites/default/files/document_library/Publications/Reports/2021/1019865/EBA%20Digital%20platforms%20report%20-%20210921.pdf

European Banking Authority. (2023a). *EU-wide stress test 2023 – Methodological note*. https://www.collegesidekick.com/study-docs/713545

European Banking Authority. (2023b). *EU-wide stress test 2023*. https://www.suerf.org/wp-content/uploads/2023/06/l_e6b4b2a746ed40e1af829d1fa82daa10_42397_suerf.pdf

European Banking Authority (2023c) 'Operational risks and resilience', in *Risk Assessment Report December 2023*. Paris: European Banking Authority, 92–106. Available at: https://www.eba.europa.eu/sites/default/files/2023-12/ed14314d-3194-4808-935b-afc564f748ad/Risk%20Assessment%20Report%20December%202023.pdf (Accessed: 2 January 2026).

European Banking Authority. (2024). *2024 Risk Assessment Report of the European Banking System*. https://www.bde.es/f/webbe/GAP/Secciones/SalaPrensa/InformacionInteres/EBA/Arc/Fic/EBA_Risk_Assessment_Report-autumn_2024.pdf

European Central Bank. (2022). SSM supervisory priorities 2023–2025. *ECB Banking Supervision*. https://www.bankingsupervision.europa.eu/framework/priorities/pdf/ssm.supervisory_priorities202212~3a1e609cf8.en.pdf

European Commission. (2018). *General Data Protection Regulation (GDPR)*. https://gdpr-info.eu/

European Commission. (2022). *Regulation (EU) 2019/2088 on sustainability-related disclosures in the financial services sector (SFDR)*. https://eur-lex.europa.eu/eli/reg/2019/2088/oj/eng

European Commission. (2023a). *Regulation (EU) 2022/2554 on digital operational resilience for the financial sector*. https://eur-lex.europa.eu/eli/reg/2022/2554/oj/eng

European Commission. (2023b). *Directive (EU) 2022/2464 on corporate sustainability reporting (CSRD)*. https://eur-lex.europa.eu/eli/dir/2022/2464/oj/eng#:~:text=Directive%20%28EU%29%202022%2F2464%20of%20the%20European%20Parliament%20and,corporate%20sustainability%20reporting%20%28Text%20with%20EEA%20relevance%29%20PE%2F35%2F2022%2FREV%2F1

European Union Agency for Cybersecurity. (2024). *ENISA threat landscape 2024*. https://www.enisa.europa.eu/publications/enisa-threat-landscape-2024

EY. (2023). *Global alternative finance report 2023*. https://www.ey.com

Federal Reserve. (2020). *Sound practices to strengthen operational resilience*. https://www.federalreserve.gov/newsevents/pressreleases/files/bcreg20201030a1.pdf

Federal Reserve. (2023). *Supervisory stress test results 2023*. https://www.federalreserve.gov/publications/files/2023-dfast-results-20230628.pdf

Financial Stability Board. (2022). *Enhancing the resilience of non-bank financial intermediation*. https://www.fsb.org/2022/11/enhancing-the-resilience-of-non-bank-financial-intermediation-progress-report-2/

Financial Stability Board. (2024). *The financial stability implications of artificial intelligence*. https://www.fsb.org/uploads/P14112024.pdf

Fonton Moffo, A. M. (2024). A machine learning approach in stress testing US bank holding companies. *International Review of Financial Analysis, 95*, Article 103476. https://doi.org/10.1016/j.irfa.2024.103476

FS-ISAC. (2023). *Navigating cyber 2023*. https://www.fsisac.com/hubfs/NavigatingCyber-2023/NavigatingCyber2023-Final.pdf?hsLang=en

International Monetary Fund (2023a) *Global Financial Stability Report, April 2023: Safeguarding financial stability amid high inflation and geopolitical risks*. Washington, DC: International Monetary Fund. Available at: https://www.imf.org/en/Publications/GFSR/Issues/2023/04/11/global-financial-stability-report-april-2023 (Accessed: 2 January 2026).

International Monetary Fund (2023b) Financial and climate policies for a high-interest-rate era. Global Financial Stability Report, October 2023. Washington, DC: International Monetary Fund. Available at: https://www.imf.org/en/Publications/GFSR/Issues/2023/10/10/global-financial-stability-report-october-2023 (Accessed: 2 January 2026)

International Monetary Fund. (2025, April 30). People's Republic of China: Financial sector assessment program—Financial system stability assessment Country Report No. 2025/100. Washington, DC: International Monetary Fund. Available at: https://www.imf.org/en/Publications/CR/Issues/2025/04/30/Peoples-Republic-of-China-Financial-Sector-Assessment-Program-Financial-System-Stability-566570 (Accessed: 2 January 2026).

International Organization of Securities Commissions. (2023). IOSCO Board priorities: Work program 2023–2024. *IOSCO*. https://www.iosco.org/library/pubdocs/pdf/IOSCOPD731.pdf

International Organization of Securities Commissions. (2025). *Artificial intelligence in capital markets: Use cases, risks and mitigants (Consultation Report)* https://www.iosco.org/library/pubdocs/pdf/IOSCOPD788.pdf

Jiang, J., Li, Y., & Wang, X. (2023). Machine learning in credit risk assessment: A survey. *Journal of Banking & Finance, 152*, 106719. https://doi.org/10.1016/j.jbankfin.2022.106719

Kopp, E., Kaffenberger, L., & Wilson, C. (2017). Cyber risk, market failures, and financial stability. IMF Working Paper WP/17/185.

KPMG. (2023). *Pulse of fintech H1 2023*. https://kpmg.com/dp/en/home/insights/2023/08/pulse-of-fintech-h1-2023.html

KPMG. (2024a). *Pulse of fintech H2 2024*. https://kpmg.com/in/en/insights/2025/03/pulse-of-fintech-h2-2024.html

KPMG. (2024b). *The race for robo advice: Building trust and accelerating growth*. KPMG Ireland. https://assets.kpmg.com/content/dam/kpmg/ie/pdf/2024/08/ie-the-race-for-robo-advice.pdf

Leitner, G., Singh, J., van der Kraaij, A., & Zsámboki, B. (2024). The rise of artificial intelligence: Benefits and risks for financial stability. *Financial Stability Review, 1*. https://ideas.repec.org/a/ecb/fsrart/202400012.html

Lessmann, S., Baesens, B., Seow, H.-V., & Thomas, L. C. (2015). Benchmarking state-of-the-art classification algorithms for credit scoring. *European Journal of Operational Research, 247*(1), 124–136. https://doi.org/10.1016/j.ejor.2015.05.030

Liu, S., Gao, L., & Chen, M. (2025). Artificial intelligence adoption and corporate financial risk. *Finance Research Letters*, *85*(Part A), Article 107938. https://doi.org/10.1016/j.frl.2025.107938

Montanaro, A. (2015). Quantum speedup of Monte Carlo methods. *Proceedings of the Royal Society A*, *471*(2181), 20150301. https://doi.org/10.1098/rspa.2015.0301

National Institute of Standards and Technology. (2024). *Post-quantum cryptography standardization (Draft FIPS 203: ML-KEM; Draft FIPS 204: ML-DSA)*. https://csrc.nist.gov/projects/post-quantum-cryptography

OECD. (2024). *Regulatory approaches to artificial intelligence in finance*. OECD Artificial Intelligence Papers, No. 24. Organisation for Economic Cooperation and Development. https://www.oecd.org/content/dam/oecd/en/publications/reports/2024/09/regulatory-approaches-to-artificial-intelligence-in-finance_43d082c3/f1498c02-en.pdf

People's Bank of China. (2021). *Progress of research & development of e-CNY in China*.

People's Bank of China (2022) 'E-CNY: Main objectives, guiding principles and inclusion considerations', *BIS Papers*, *123*, 45–48. Available at: https://www.bis.org/publ/bppdf/bispap123_e.pdf (Accessed: 2 January 2026).

PwC. (2022). Charting a course amid evolution and revolution: PwC future of payments. *PricewaterhouseCoopers*. https://www.pwc.com/gx/en/financial-services/fs-2025/pwc-future-of-payments.pdf

Rojas, H., & Dias, D. (2018). Transmission of macroeconomic shocks to risk parameters: Their uses in stress testing. *arXiv*. https://doi.org/10.48550/arXiv.1809.07401

Rudin, C. (2019). Stop explaining black box machine learning models for high-stakes decisions and use interpretable models instead. *Nature Machine Intelligence*, *1*(5), 206–215. https://doi.org/10.1038/s42256-019-0048-x

Saavedra, L. R. S., Gomes, A. L., de Castro Gomes, A. P., & Kimura, H. (2024) 'Probability of default for lifetime credit loss for IFRS 9 using machine learning competing risks survival analysis models', *Expert Systems with Applications*, 242, 123607. https://doi.org/10.1016/j.eswa.2024.123607

State Council of the People's Republic of China. (2023, March 16). *China releases plan on reforming party and state institutions*. The State Council Information Office of the PRC. https://english.www.gov.cn/policies/latestreleases/202303/16/content_WS6413be82c6d0f528699db58e.html

Task Force on Climate-related Financial Disclosures (2023) 2023 Status Report. Basel: Financial Stability Board. Available at: https://www.fsb.org/uploads/P121023-2.pdf (accessed 1 January 2026)

U.S. Department of the Treasury. (2022). Financial Stability Oversight Council annual report 2022. https://home.treasury.gov/system/files/261/FSOC2022AnnualReport.pdf

Woerner, S., & Egger, D. J. (2019). Quantum risk analysis. *NPJ Quantum Information*, *5*, 15. https://doi.org/10.1038/s41534-019-0130-6

World Bank. (2019). Blockchain in financial services in emerging markets, Part I. *World Bank Group*. https://openknowledge.worldbank.org/entities/publication/12b4d788-dbec-5a29-b323-186684800729

World Bank. (2020). Cybersecurity and financial stability: How cyber risk can destabilize the financial system. *World Bank Group*. https://openknowledge.worldbank.org/entities/publication/13d4e8f0-57f3-5c45-b6de-9447302c8e7e

Zetzsche, D. A., Buckley, R. P., Arner, D. W., & Barberis, J. N. (2020). Regulating digital finance. *European Economy – Banks, Regulation, and the Real Sector*, *3*(2), 95–122.

7 Conclusion

Bruno S. Sergi

As global shocks, from pandemics and wars to climate disasters and digital upheaval, multiply in frequency and intensity, financial resilience has vaulted to the top of policy and boardroom agendas. Yet, too often, it is reduced to regulatory checklists: Basel buffers here and stress tests there. True resilience is far richer. It is the capacity to absorb shocks, adapt operations, and emerge stronger, not merely recover to a prior state but evolve in response to new realities. The following overview, drawn from interlocking chapters, presents a comprehensive blueprint for resilience that spans households and multinationals, data centers, and village savings clubs, among others. This blueprint serves as a clear roadmap for all stakeholders, providing a detailed guide on enhancing financial resilience. Among the factors that significantly affect the financial resilience of financial institutions are, among others, climate change and environment-related risks, as well as social risk and governance, which directly affect financial institutions but also act indirectly by influencing the financial situation of entities—clients of financial institutions.

Financial resilience demands a systemic approach that unites households and corporates, prudential buffers, green bonds, digital firewalls, and social networks. Policymakers must streamline regulations; incentivize resilience-enhancing investments in digital infrastructure, human-capital development, and community-based financial literacy; and foster global data-sharing and early-warning alliances. Financial institutions must commit leadership attention and resources to embed resilience thinking in every process, from product design to board-level strategy. Academia and think tanks should refine multidimensional metrics that capture shock absorption and adaptive evolution. In a world where fragility anywhere can trigger contagion everywhere, bolstering our financial systems is both an economic imperative. By embracing a holistic roadmap and anchoring prudential strength in people, planet, and technology, it is possible to withstand the next crisis and emerge transformed and more robust for whatever storms lie ahead.

DOI: 10.4324/9781003648840-7

Index

Pages in *italics* refer to figures and pages in **bold** refer to tables.

Absorption of shocks 27–28, **29**
adaptation 19–20
asset quality (NPLs, IFRS 9) 8–15, **15–16**

Bank exposures to climate risks 19
banking 20
Banking and Insurance Regulatory Commission (CBIRC) 97, 103
Basel II 8–9
Basel III **34**
BCBS recommendations 10
Basel I regulations 8
Behavioral sciences 20
business continuity (BCP/DRP) **38**
business models 92

Capital (capital adequacy) 97
capital buffers 6, 9, 12
Capital ratio 9–14, **15**
Capital Requirements Directive (CRD) Directives 8
Capital Requirements Regulation 11
central bank credibility **29**
climate science 3, 20
Commercial and residential real-estate markets (CRE and RRE) 31
Computer science 3
corporate governance **29**
Countercyclical Capital Buffer (CCyB) 11, 13, **16**, **18**
CRD/CRR **29**
CRISK index 19
CSRD **29**
cyberattacks **30**

Determinants of the Financial Resilience of Financial Institutions **29–30**
Digital Operational Resilience Act (DORA) 3, 103
diversification of income sources **29**

ECB 103–104
energy transition **30**, 39, 46, 51, 54, 65
Environmental, Social, and Governance 47, 70–71, 78
Equity Tier 9, 87
ESG practices 72, 76
ESG ratings 78
ESG risk 2
ESG risks into ERM **29**
EU Taxonomy **29**, **34**, 36, **38**, *90*, 91, **102**, 103
extreme weather events **30**, 75

financial crisis (2008) 6, 31, 89, *90*
financial planning 7, 77
financial resilience 7
financial shocks 6–7

financial stability 6
Financial System Stability and Resilience 27
financial-market participants 26
Fintech 63

geopolitical uncertainty 67

Insurers 3, 26, **29**

lending 78
Leverage Ratio 9, 87
Liquidity Coverage Ratio 13
liquidity (LCR, NSFR, contingency funding) 12
Life-Cycle Hypothesis 2, 6
LTV ratios **30**

machine learning 92
monetary policy **29–30**

net stable funding ratio 87
NGFS **29**, **34**, 35
non-bank entities and fintechs 26
non-bank financial institutions (NBFIs) 31

outsourcing 11, **34–35**
OECD framework for financial well-being and resilience 7

pension funds (coverage of liabilities) **29**

RAF **29**, **38**
RAG terms 14
reporting and measurement of ESG 79–81
risk culture **29**
resilience of financial institutions 29

SFDR **29**
Solvency II **29**
specifically, the collapse of Bankhaus Herstatt in Germany in 1974 8
stranded-asset risk **30**
SupTech/RegTech monitoring **30**
sustainability **38**

TCFD 80
technologies 92–98
theory of "buffer-stock" behavior 7
Threat-Led Penetration Testing (TLPT) for critical functions 11
tokenisation and DLT risks **30**
transition **30**, 31–33, **34–35**